9/07

PATRON SAINTS

PATRON SAINTS

HOW THE SAINTS GAVE NEW ORLEANS A REASON TO BELIEVE

ALAN DONNES

CENTER STREET®

NEW YORK BOSTON NASHVILLE

This book is not sanctioned by the NFL or the New Orleans Saints.

Center Street
Hachette Book Group USA
237 Park Avenue
New York, NY 10017

Visit our Web site at www.centerstreet.com.

Center Street is a division of Hachette Book Group USA, Inc.
The Center Street name and logo is a trademark of Hachette Book Group USA, Inc.
Printed in the United States of America

First Edition: September 2007
10 9 8 7 6 5 4 3 2 1

Library of Congress Cataloging-in-Publication Data
Donnes, Alan.
    Patron Saints : how the Saints gave New Orleans a reason to believe /
Alan Donnes.
        p.   cm.
    ISBN-13: 978-1-59995-017-4
    ISBN-10: 1-59995-017-0
    1. New Orleans Saints (Football team)   2. Football—Social aspects—
Louisiana—New Orleans.   3. Hurricane Katrina, 2005.   I. Title.

GV956.N366D66   2007
796.332'640976335—dc22
                                2007021001

In memory of
Buddy Diliberto,
Wayne Mack,
my good friend Ricky Stockner,
and all the other Saints fans who are no longer with us.

CONTENTS

CONTENTS

FOREWORD
BY CHRIS MEYERS

THERE I STOOD, my feet ice-cold in the snow, covering the Saints' sideline for FOX Sports on a wintry day in Chicago. My focus was on my work, but my heart drifted like a flurry of snowflakes to some two decades earlier when I had stood on the floor of the Superdome as the franchise went to its first-ever play-off. The cheers from the hometown crowd were deafening then. The team had become the pulse of the city.

But that day in Chicago, and that whole past year, New Orleans wasn't the same. The city and the whole Gulf region were still recovering from the devastation of Hurricane Katrina, a violent storm that had shown no mercy to a place I once called home, a place full of people who always knew how to have a good time, or would *laissez le bon temps roulez*, as they say.

But these were tragic times. The Superdome, the very place

where the Saints had evoked such extreme emotion, was a beaten-down symbol of something that had ripped the heart out of the Crescent City. The Saints, a team without a true home, a team rumored to be moving because conditions were just that bad, suddenly became America's adopted underdogs.

I saw it with my own eyes, traveling the country, covering the NFL. I felt it when fans and players from distant places and opposing teams rooted openly for the Saints, even though they weren't their own team. They were rooting for New Orleans, for its people and its recovery.

It was clear that the anchor of all this was the Saints, a group of men who toughed it out, who stuck together, who dug in and helped out. They were a football team, not just any team, but a team that in the past had been as unreliable as the weather, a team that had been made fun of so much they had become a punch line. But this was not the same old city, and these were not the same old Saints. You could count on them this time—you could believe. They provided hope. And they showed that anything is possible. To go from a 3–13 season to a division title and the NFC Championship game proved it.

Sports teams have always represented their cities well, but the weight that the Saints carried this year was huge. Never before has a team with such history rallied an entire region of the country in such a short time. I witnessed a disappointing Saints defeat that day, but after what they and their fans had endured, surely this time was good enough.

Patron Saints captures all the grit and heart of that remarkable year. In its pages you'll find stories of tragedy and of triumph, and when you read it you will feel the same emotion and drama that the people of New Orleans and sports fans everywhere felt.

INTRODUCTION

I WAS FIVE years old when Pete Rozelle made the announcement that New Orleans had a football team. It was All Saints' Day, so I was probably at Greenwood Cemetery with my family, whitewashing our family tombs and eating some of the candy I had been given during the previous night's trick-or-treating. Maybe Hale Boggs, Russell Long, and Dave Dixon tricked Rozelle, but I, like a lot of people, would be treated to some incredible memories.

My dad got season tickets for my two older brothers and me. Youth seats were $1.50 back then, and we had north end zone seats right behind the scoreboard. We could put our drinks and popcorn on it like a coffee table. I have a lot of memories of the Saints at old Tulane Stadium. One of my fondest was racing down the ramps all the way from the upper deck just before the end of the halves to watch the players walk by.

The Saints had built locker rooms outside of the stadium. Players from both teams would come off the field and then walk through barricades covered with fans to get to them. My friends and I would stand on the barricades and, with arms and hands reaching out, try to pat one of the players on his back. We'd shout "good game," regardless of the score, in the hope that one of them would toss us a highly prized, game-worn sweatband. I got one once, and I wore it proudly every chance I had.

One time, a classmate came to school with Archie Manning's autograph. It was on a plain white paper napkin his parents had begged Archie to sign during a chance meeting somewhere. That kid ruled the schoolyard, and we all asked just to see it. A week later it was my chance to reign supreme, when my mom bought me an official Archie Manning #8 sweatshirt. I wore it for years until I literally split the seams. In neighborhood football games played on the Fleur-de-Lis neutral ground, I'd wear it and play quarterback. I would roll out to throw or scramble, because I was Archie Manning. Of course, if we decided to go for three, I was Tom Dempsey. I'd line up and kick the ball over the electrical wires.

Win or lose, the Saints were my heroes. We had no idea how much they were paid, unlike today when it seems that the most important statistic to many players is their salary. Maybe that mattered to our Saints back then, too, but we never knew and we were better for it. We had undisputed heroes.

When I was back home in New Orleans visiting after Hurricane Katrina, I drove down 12th Street, past where my childhood home had been. It was gone, erased by the water and the winds. So much of what I knew as a young boy growing up in New Orleans was lost, but as I turned onto Fleur-de-Lis Drive, there was the neutral ground and there were the electrical wires. The memories of the games played there came rushing back, and with them came memories of my Saintly heroes.

When I began conducting interviews for this book, I had hoped that these Saints would be heroes, too, and they were. With each interview it became more and more apparent that what they had done for the people—my people—was much bigger than the game of football. At a time when New Orleans needed heroes, they had become them. In this book you won't find contract dollars or a lot of statistics; let somebody else write that book. What you will find are memories of what it was like to be here during this unique period of time in a very special place we call home. The voices heard here are not just the selected memories of a chosen few; rather, they represent the shared memories of every player and every fan who ever lived here or wished they had.

To each and every one of you, wherever you are, thanks for being in that number.

PATRON SAINTS

"These people need hope. We it."
—Saints owner Tom Benson,
in the wake of Hurricane Katrina

COME HELL AND HIGH WATER

MONDAY, AUGUST 29, 2006, will long be remembered as the darkest day in the history of New Orleans and the Gulf Coast region. In the early morning hours a massive hurricane named Katrina, swollen to epic proportions by the warm waters of the Gulf of Mexico, paid us a most unwelcome visit. At first, the storm passed and the damage seemed at least manageable, no worse than normal in the course of life in Hurricane Alley. Then the levees broke.

In the days that followed, the catastrophic aftermath of the storm was seared into the nation's collective memory. On the Gulf Coast, whole towns were simply wiped off the map. In New Orleans, entire neighborhoods were destroyed, houses simply picked up and carried away. Thousands of residents languished in hospitals and nursing homes with no power. Thousands more were left stranded on rooftops and at the Superdome and Convention Center. They had no food, no water, and no way to escape. Once the full measure of the storm's wreckage was assessed, over $80 billion in damage had been done and nearly

2,000 people had lost their lives. It was the worst natural disaster in American history.

But three days earlier, death and destruction were the furthest things from anyone's mind. Hurricane Katrina was just a minor storm somewhere off in the Gulf of Mexico, and the people of New Orleans had their attention fixed on a much higher priority: football.

That night, led by quarterback Aaron Brooks and head coach Jim Haslett, the New Orleans Saints were about to take on the Baltimore Ravens in a routine preseason matchup. The fans in attendance filtered into the Superdome, laughing and having a good time, buying their beer and hot dogs, settling in for the big game. Outside the dome, still more Saints devotees gathered with friends around big-screen TVs at their local bars, celebrating their team in the best local tradition. Others around the city tuned in their radios and car stereos to the game broadcast on WWL and waited to see what the Saints would do. And when the team took to the field that night, everything seemed perfectly normal. A few scattered weather reports were the only clues that their destiny was about to change forever.

Kenny Wilkerson, *sideline reporter, WWL Radio*

It was a pretty good crowd for a preseason game, and it was pretty relaxed early on. Everybody knew before the Ravens game that there was a hurricane out somewhere off the tip of Florida. It wasn't that nobody was watching it, but at the time it was a category one, and it was supposed to hit Florida. If you live in New Orleans or anywhere along the coast, you see a couple of these every year. I mean, nobody had any idea it would become what it became.

Sammy Marten, *fan*

I was watching the game on TV, and they took one of those breaks for news. The guys said that Katrina was changing course and was heading for either Louisiana or Mississippi. I'm up in Memphis, but I have family all down around there. I wasn't real worried, though.

Bobby Hebert, *former quarterback, New Orleans Saints*

Before the game, the weather people had been talking about this hurricane down near Miami, but it was still supposed to go up into Florida. So, we knew about it in the radio studio, but we didn't really talk about it while we were doing the pregame show. They did in the news, but not so much during the Saints coverage. You know, down here, this time of year, we're more concerned with football than with some hurricane going to Florida.

Jack Catilanotta, *fan*

My wife, Dale, and I were out with friends at Parkway Bakery, a great little bar and café. We were eating po'boys and dancing to a band called New Orleans Streetcar. It was one of those magical New Orleans nights. The place was crowded, and everyone was "passing a good time," as we say down here.

They had the Saints game on the television, and all of a sudden, I remember local weatherman Carl Arredondo cutting into the game, saying that a major shift in the storm known as Katrina had taken place. It was now taking a direct course for New Orleans.

Before you knew it, cell phones were going off all over the patio, and everybody's facial expressions slowly started taking on this weird sense of urgency. It was that age-old question: Do we evacuate?

Pam Randazza, *owner, Black & Gold Sports Shop*

I was in my seat at the dome, watching the game. Everybody's cell phones started ringing at the same time. It was weird. Then people started grabbing their things and heading for the exits.

Kenny Wilkerson

You could see that people were all getting told about it. Then they made an announcement over the stadium PA. It wasn't a panic, but you could tell something was happening. And, nothing to do with the hurricane, but the team didn't look real good that night. They lost 21–6. The Superdome emptied out real fast.

Bobby Hebert

Usually, all we talk about after the game is the Saints, but I was giving out coordinates. I was giving the longitudes and the latitudes of the storm, estimated times for landfall, all that stuff—on a sports show. By the end of the broadcast, it was almost all about the hurricane.

I still have a house in Atlanta, so that's where I was going. I wasn't going to be here for this one. It was going to be bad.

Mickey Loomis, *general manager, New Orleans Saints*

We told all of our players, "Listen, spend all of Saturday and Sunday morning getting your family out of harm's way. Then report to Saints headquarters at noon on Sunday."

The plan was once we got everybody there, we'd go to the airport and fly to San Jose. We had our next preseason game against Oakland the following week.

We set up a call center in New Orleans before we left. We made sure that every player had a way to get their family out of town. We had a few players that didn't, so we matched them up with other spouses and family members. We just made sure that everybody had (a) a way to get out and (b) a place to go.

Brian Grenrood, *news director, FOX 8*

About fifteen of us volunteered to man the TV station during the hurricane. I was the news director, so I sort of needed to be there. We had evacuated most of the staff to Mobile earlier in the day. I think at first they didn't believe it was going to be that bad. As the storm got closer, it was so big and so strong that you knew things were going to be rough. We were battening down the hatches, and I planned to ride it out at the station.

Michelle Babineaux, *owner, Michaul's Cajun Dance Hall*

I took my son and we got out of there. I locked up my restaurant and we got out of the city. I live in Venetian Isles, which is east of the city. It's right on the water, actually between the levee and the lake. So how crazy am I? Let me tell you, though, I might be crazy to live there, but I'm not stupid. I took my son, and we left.

Abbe Garfinkel, *fan*

I kept hoping that it would miss us, but then I saw on television how big it was. It was as big as the Gulf of Mexico. I said, "We're going."

We have dogs, and I wasn't going to leave them behind, so we needed a hotel that would take them. We also wanted to go somewhere that would be far enough away from landfall that we would have electricity after the storm. We had stayed at the Ramada Inn in Natchez, Mississippi, before. They had let us keep the dogs with us, so that was where we headed. We called ahead, and they said that they were booked. I said, "Well, we're coming, and if anything becomes available, hold it for us."

Mickey Loomis

The players and the coaches all took care of their families. We met at the facility on Sunday, got on the plane, and really, just wished and hoped for the best.

Abbe Garfinkel

We got to Natchez and they said that, no, they didn't have a room, and that the nearest one they knew of was in Dallas. Dallas? I said, "Thanks, but I'm not driving to Dallas. I'll be out in the parking lot. We'll wait in the car, and if somebody doesn't show up or if you have anything at all, we'll take it." And I went back out and sat in my car.

Brian Grenrood

At about 10 p.m., FOX corporate called and ordered all of us to leave. They said, "If you stay, you're fired."

Well, because we had all planned on being at the station, none of us had anywhere to go. We all called around frantically trying to find places where we could ride out the storm. I was supposed to go to the Kenner Police Station with three other guys, but we all thought better about it and decided to just fend for ourselves.

My wife was in Lake Charles. I decided to drive and meet her there. My car was low on gas, and of course, the gas stations were all closed by then. The owners had all evacuated and boarded them up. I had to go to my mother-in-law's house and get her car to make the drive. I didn't get on the interstate until after 11 p.m., and it was deserted.

Driving west toward Lake Charles you have to drive over a long bridge that goes over the Bonnet Carre Spillway. Lake Pontchartrain is immediately to your right as you drive over it. By then the winds were over fifty miles per hour, and I had to hold the steering wheel tightly with both hands just to keep the car on the road. Between New Orleans and Baton Rouge I saw a total of two other cars, both heading out.

Abbe Garfinkel

I went back in to the motel at about three or four in the morning. They told me that they still didn't have anything but that we were welcome to come in and wait in the lounge. They were remodeling it, and so it was sort of torn up, but there was a TV in there, and we could try to get comfortable. I told them about the dogs, and they said that it was okay to bring them inside. They were really so nice.

So, we went in and made a little area for us and the dogs. We lay across some chairs and started watching the Weather Channel. As we were watching I just kept thinking, what is going to happen? What is going to be left when we get back?

Michelle Babineaux

I just watched and hoped that maybe it would turn at the last minute or we'd have some kind of miracle. I hoped I'd have a house when I got back. That was all I could do—hope and pray.

YOU GOTTA HAVE FAITH

WHEN THE LEVEES broke and a swollen Lake Pontchartrain surged forth into the streets of New Orleans, America felt a ripple effect from coast to coast. Waves of evacuees washed ashore in every place imaginable. They fled by the thousands to the largest nearby cities, Baton Rouge and Lafayette. They trickled by the dozens into little Cajun towns like Abbeville and Mamou. Plucked from atop their roofs and out of the floodwaters, they scattered to places as far away as Seattle, Detroit, and New York.

The greatest number by far found themselves in Houston, Texas, thanks to the long-delayed rescue of those stranded at the Superdome and the Convention Center. Crammed onto the floor of the Astrodome, these evacuees represented the poorest, most tragic cases to be found. Families had been torn apart. Seniors and invalids had been left to fend for themselves. Children wandered the floor of the arena, alone.

Unable to return, these evacuees watched on television as their beloved city fell to the rising tide. The damage inflicted by the storm was staggering. There was no doubt about what Katrina had done to the city, indeed to the entire Gulf Coast. But each and every person watching from afar was gripped by crippling uncertainties. Are my loved ones okay? Did my home survive? What will be left for me when I return? Even the Saints, marooned in San Jose, California, looked to their home, the Superdome, and wondered what its fate would be.

With so many questions in the air, confusion reigned. The charitable outpouring of the country was swift and immense, but the waiting and the suffering continued. With nothing concrete on which to peg their hopes, the only thing the people of New Orleans had left, it seemed, was faith.

Pam Randazza, *owner, Black & Gold Sports Shop*

I run the Black & Gold Sports Shop, the official New Orleans Saints merchandise store. Just before the team got started with the 2005 season—before Katrina hit or any of it—their marketing people called me and said that the theme for that season was going to be "Faith." They have a theme like that every year, and this year that was it. They had finished on a high note last season, winning four games in a row, and so it was like they were saying, "Have faith. We're going to do it this year."

They told me, "You really ought to get behind this." So I did. We ordered a lot of T-shirts and other gear with nothing but a great big fleur-de-lis and the word "FAITH" in big letters.

Can you believe it? At the time nobody knew what was coming, but boy, that's what everybody was going to need: faith.

Mickey Loomis, *general manager, New Orleans Saints*

The year before, 2004, we had evacuated the team to San Antonio for another hurricane, because there was a threat that it would hit New Orleans. That one ended up taking a sharp turn east and missing the city, but there had been a mandatory evacuation and we'd taken the team there for two or three days. So, we had been through this before.

I had spoken to some city officials in prior years, and one guy told me that if a category four or five hurricane ever hit New Orleans head-on, there would be 70,000 dead people. That kind of catches your ear. I remember thinking at the time, okay, if there is ever the threat of a hurricane I will get my family out of here, even if it's just a threat, even if the evacuation isn't mandatory.

Joe Horn, *wide receiver, New Orleans Saints*

They had always said that if a hurricane went right at the city, New Orleans would be destroyed and thousands of people would die. Still, you never really think it will happen. Never in any nightmare did I think anything as apocalyptic as Katrina would take place. I was more than shocked. When I saw what was happening, I just went numb all over. "Oh no," I thought. "This ain't real. This ain't happening."

Quint Davis, *producer and founder, New Orleans Jazz & Heritage Festival*

I was lying in bed in New York watching CNN and they had a nurse from Charity Hospital on. She was saying that there was flooding around there. At first I figured the streets must be flooding from the rain, but then she said that the water was really high. I thought, that much water? By Charity? That's downtown. That's by the Superdome. How can that be?

Then it sunk in: Oh my God, the levees have broken. Oh my God, oh my God.

Michael Lewis, *kick return specialist, New Orleans Saints*

I slept only for like an hour that night, if that. I watched everything I could on TV. I had the Weather Channel on all night.

Abbe Garfinkel, *fan*

After spending most of the night in my car, I went to the desk clerk and said, "You must have at least one room here that we can have. Maybe a room that isn't that nice or something?"

They said, "Well, we have one with no furniture."

It was part of a suite or something, and it didn't have any beds.

I asked, "Does it have a bathroom and a floor?"

"Yes."

"We'll take it."

I was in the checkout line at Wal-Mart buying air mattresses when they called and said, "Come quick, we have a real room opening up."

I put them away and rushed back. We checked in, and later we were all watching television. We turned to the Weather Channel, and the storm was over—it had passed. But they were still talking about rising water in New Orleans. "What are they talking about? What's going on?" We couldn't believe it.

There was flooding on Canal Street. They showed the Saenger Theatre, and it was inundated. I used to work there. After that it was just a horror show. You couldn't watch it, and you couldn't not watch it. We just kept screaming at the television, "Plug the holes! Plug the holes!"

Well, we lived at the Ramada for two weeks.

Michelle Babineaux, *owner, Michaul's Cajun Dance Hall*

When I saw everything on TV, well, I just knew that my house was going to be in bad shape. I ended up with twenty-two feet of water in my house.

Mickey Loomis

Everyone knew that the storm was going to hit sometime Monday. We had a plan, but we were caught off guard. We had the game against the Ravens Friday night. At that point, Jefferson Parish had ordered a mandatory evacuation, but New Orleans had not.

All the Saints executives met Saturday morning and decided that we were going to round up the team and fly to San Jose, California. We could spend Monday, Tuesday, Wednesday, and Thursday in San Jose and then play our game Thursday night against Oakland. Then we'd be back in New Orleans on Friday. So we were prepared. We had a disaster plan; we had always had one. But having a plan and actually implementing a plan are two different things.

Joe Horn

My first reaction was shock and awe. I was in shock. I was in awe. The most devastating thing for me was the people walking waist-high in the water. The devastation wasn't just the flooding of the buildings and the houses. It was the people. When you see people on the roofs of their houses, with babies and stuff, people just trying to survive. That's what had the whole world gasping for air.

Anthony Canatella, *deputy superintendent, New Orleans Police Department*

When the storm hit, I was the commander of the Sixth District, so I was at the police station there on Martin Luther King [Jr.] Blvd. Total chaos. There was no water, no food, no electricity.

There was no way to communicate, either. Nobody knew what was going on, because we couldn't talk to each other. We didn't know where a lot of our officers were or how to contact them. It was a really bad situation until the military arrived and started to get things more under control.

Kenny Wilkerson, *sideline reporter, WWL Radio*

I was lucky, I live on a good bit of land, and we have these big tall pine trees all around the house. A couple of them fell, but they fell in such a way that not one of them touched the house. There was no flooding, either, so I was really lucky. I couldn't believe what I was seeing on TV, just couldn't comprehend it, but I knew how lucky my wife and I were.

Mickey Loomis

We didn't have a long-term plan, just a short-term plan. How would you even draw up a plan for something like this? We had a place to practice—San Jose State let us use their facilities—and we had a place to stay for the week, so at least we were set for the time being.

They kept showing the Superdome, the big holes in the roof and all of the people down there and the horror of what was happening. I think anybody would forget about football for a bit and just try to absorb what was happening. I know I did.

Quint Davis

They kept showing the Superdome all torn up. It was horrible to see people living like that. I wanted to do something; I think everybody wanted to do something, but you didn't even know where to start. You couldn't get through to anybody, the phones and electricity were not working down there. You couldn't talk to anybody even to see what you could do.

Kenny Wilkerson

We didn't do a broadcast for the preseason Oakland Raiders game that week. We just couldn't. WWL couldn't even find the staff we needed to do the broadcast. The airport was shut down, and so we couldn't have gotten to Oakland anyway. A lot of people didn't even have electricity to listen to the game, and quite honestly, I think they had more pressing needs than listening to a preseason game. They were still trying to get home and find their families.

I don't know how the Saints played that game. All the guys on the team had wives and houses back here, so they had to be thinking about all of that. I wasn't there, but they had a moment of silence before the game. Afterwards, a lot of the players had a prayer circle out on the field. They played their best, but they lost 13–6.

Mickey Loomis

It was overwhelming for a good many of our guys. By that time, I think our players at least knew that their families were safe. Once you know that, then it's time to go back to work, which for them meant playing football. What was overwhelming was what was going on back in Louisiana, Mississippi, and the entire Gulf Coast.

Joe Horn

We couldn't go back to New Orleans, so they took us to San Antonio. As soon as we got there, I knew I needed to go to Houston and see what I could do to help those people. They had brought thousands and thousands of people from Louisiana, my people, to the Astrodome. So, when we got to San Antonio, the very next morning, I hired a car to take my friend Terence Rice and me to Houston. I got up at six o'clock, took a shower, and went straight there. That was my deal. I wanted to get hands-on with these people.

When I got there, it was just so terrible. All these people, they were all crowded into this place and given cots, but they didn't know where their families were. They didn't know who was alive and who was dead. So many had been taken to the Astrodome, but maybe their sister or their mother was taken somewhere else, like Utah or some other far-off place. They were scared and very many of them just looked lost, broken, I guess.

There were old people there. I am talking about eighty-, ninety-year-old people there by themselves without anybody but strangers. Maybe they had a little paper bag or something with a few things in it, and that was all they had in the world. There were children without their families, just put on a cot and given something to eat.

Look, I don't mean this in a bad way, but my perception was that they were being treated like animals in a kennel. "Here's something to eat and a place to sleep. Stay there, and we'll catch you when we can catch you." It was so upsetting. It was tearing me up inside, but I knew I had to be strong for them.

I cried. I tried not to, but I cried. I had to go behind these security walls to let my emotions run through me; I didn't want the kids, the people, to see me break down. I went behind that wall a few times and just broke down.

I went to a lot of places to try to help where I could. Wal-Mart had a lot of cameras that caught me there. I didn't arrange to have any press there; they were just there. The people at Wal-Mart needed things, basic things—*everything*. Pampers, milk, toothbrushes, deodorant, baby oil, pots, pans, money, whatever. You name it. They were grateful for whatever they could get.

You gotta understand, these people had their whole lives, everything in their homes, taken away. They had nothing. They didn't have a pot to piss in. They were in unfamiliar territory. People were telling them, "We want to help you," but they didn't have anything to give them. So, the first person they saw that they recognized, like myself or the other players, they had to swallow their pride and ask for help. People had to swallow their pride because they knew that they might not see Ernie Conwell again. "I may not see Joe Horn. I may not see Willie Whitehead, Michael Lewis, or Deuce McAllister again, so while I have the opportunity to get a few dollars to take care of my family or to get soap or water or whatever, I need to ask for it. These volunteers are doing the best they can, but they might not have the necessities that one of these Saints players can get for me."

So I went up to the cashiers at the front of the Wal-Mart and I gave them my credit card and I said, "Give these people whatever they need." Then, the players who were there with me, they did the same thing.

There were a lot of people, celebrities, who were sending money to the Red Cross and this fund or that fund, but I think the people needed more than that. Sometimes it's not about the money. Sometimes it's about people sitting down and saying "You know what, Mr. Horn? You came here and I would like to tell you what happened to my family, what I did."

Sitting down and having these conversations with people, money never even came up. They were happy just for me to be there to give them a hug. Children were running up and hugging me, saying "Joe, we love you. Thanks for coming out here."

That right there made their day. It let them know we cared, really cared. I'm not saying that people who gave money did a bad thing by not coming. Maybe they couldn't come, but I think us players being there and talking to the kids made them less afraid. They needed an ear. They needed someone to hear what they went through. They needed someone to get them thinking that they would be okay.

As much as the Saints had been thrown into chaos and disarray, the business of the National Football League is football, and so the league and the team had to make some very quick and difficult decisions. Almost immediately, the game against the Giants—scheduled for September 18 at the now unusable Superdome—was moved to the Meadowlands. Saints owner Tom Benson and Giants owner Wellington Mara donated a large portion of the gate proceeds to hurricane relief efforts. Their contribution, combined with that of the NFL Players Association, raised more than $2.4 million. This would be just the first of many efforts by NFL teams and their fans to assist and support efforts along the Gulf Coast.

The NFL designated the second weekend of the new season as Hurricane Relief Weekend. They conducted an unprecedented telethon featuring some of the biggest names, past and present, ever to play the game. Under the theme of "Recover and Rebuild," the NFL, its teams and television partners used the weekend's games to raise money and bring awareness to the massive needs of Katrina's victims. The impact was both immediate and long-lasting. At a time when many question the examples set by those in professional sports, the NFL, the Saints, and their fans were setting new standards of integrity.

Brian McCarthy, *director of communications, National Football League*

The NFL is about the twin pillars of football and community. Our role is to be leaders in the community and to use our unique ability to bring people together to help others. And so after Katrina, we were using the popularity of the league, the teams, and players to help generate funds and exposure for the Gulf Coast region.

NFL owners, players, and fans have generated over $22 million and counting to help the Gulf Coast recovery process. The league committed an additional $15 million to the renovation of the Superdome. We have raised money through player and owner donations, asking fans to donate at stadiums and through the telethon held in conjunction with the Saints–Giants game.

After the devastation of Hurricane Katrina, it was important that the team and the league play a role in lifting the spirit of the community while assisting in the recovery and relief efforts. It was not a time to walk away from the people of New Orleans. It was a time to walk *with* the people of New Orleans, and that's what the Saints did.

Pam Randazza

Once I got back to the city and opened the Black & Gold Shop back up, I had no idea what to expect. There were no home games, of course. Most of the people were still gone. Other than a handful of folks who hadn't lost their homes, the only people here were FEMA workers, National Guard troops, and all these laborers coming in to help start the cleanup.

But then a funny thing happened. All the gear I had for the 2005 season—all the shirts and the hats with "FAITH" and the fleur-de-lis on them—I started selling it, a lot of it. All the workers and cleanup crews, they started wearing these shirts that just simply said "FAITH." It was like a symbol, a statement. It was like we were telling the world, "We still believe."

3

WHEN THE SAINTS CAME MARCHING IN

WHEN YOU LOOK at the relationship between a professional sports franchise and the city it calls home, it's always rocky. Fans are quick to rail against "the bums" for a losing season. Local sportswriters look for the juicy angle on a story, taking shots at owners and managers because it makes good copy. And of course there's always some overzealous activist looking to blame all the city's social ills on our national obsession with professional sports. But that only happens when there's no thought that the team might *actually leave*. Football and community. It's something we take for granted.

In the wake of Hurricane Katrina, the special bond between New Orleans and its team looked as if it might be broken forever. The Superdome was in ruins, and many of the fans simply gone. Would the Saints come back? Should they come back? No one knew.

To understand just how much was at stake, to see just what the loss of the Saints would mean, you have to go back to the beginning. Today, creating or moving a major sports franchise is a somewhat corporate affair, but the origins of the Saints are inextricably tied to the spirit and the people who make New Orleans what it is.

On November 1, 1966—All Saints' Day, by no coincidence—NFL Commissioner Pete Rozelle stepped up to a podium in the ballroom of the Pontchartrain Hotel on New Orleans's historic St. Charles Avenue. Here in the picturesque Garden District, where little had changed for over a century, reporters gathered to hear his address, one that would bring the city roaring into the modern age. Rozelle announced to thunderous applause what had been rumored for months: "Professional football has voted a franchise to the state of Louisiana and the city of New Orleans."

The local newspaper, the *New Orleans States-Item*, proclaimed in a banner headline: "N. O. GOES PRO!!!" And indeed it had. With Rozelle's announcement, New Orleans joined the ranks of New York, Chicago, and Los Angeles—major cities that boasted NFL teams. For much of our nation's history, New Orleans had been one of the largest, most important, and most strategic cities in North America. Its standing had since diminished, but New Orleans could now consider itself part of the big leagues once again.

Down here, "lagniappe" is a word that means "a little bit more," something extra and unexpected thrown in. Everything here seems to have a little lagniappe, and the story of how New Orleans got an NFL franchise is no different.

Dave Dixon, *"Father of the Superdome"*

The story of the Saints goes back further than most people realize. You see, Chep Morrison, who was mayor from '46 to '61, announced that he wanted to get a Major League Baseball team for New Orleans and build a baseball park out near the Lakefront. Well, I knew that New Orleans was a football city and not really a baseball town.

So, I called him and told him, "You have the wrong sport and the wrong stadium. People in New Orleans love football." We had LSU, and they were packed. Heck, you could get 30,000 or more just to watch a high school game, and then there was Tulane. They were drawing well, too. We also had the Sugar Bowl every year, and that game is one of the biggest in all of college football.

I told him what we needed was a professional football team, and that we should build an indoor stadium right downtown. I had been researching this for a long time. I knew that professional football would do blockbuster business here. The sport was getting more popular every year.

Immediately—and I mean immediately—he put me on the professional sports committee. From that day on I went to work to get a team here.

Lindy Boggs, *widow of U.S. Representative Hale Boggs*

First of all, Louisiana was very fortunate that Senator Russell Long was the majority whip in the Senate, and Hale Boggs, my husband, was the majority whip in the House of Representatives. The whip controls what comes to the floor of the House and the Senate. Hale and Russell were also on the sister committees of finance and ways and means.

So, what they basically were able to do was get the league to expand—but only by one team, and only *if* that team came to New Orleans. So that was, in a nutshell, what happened. Together, they were just that powerful at that time.

Dave Dixon

Just a short time before we got the team, the NFL and the AFL had agreed to merge, and that was a very big deal. That merger would create a monopoly, in effect, on pro football, and so it raised a lot of concerns about antitrust and so forth. All the bidding on players that had gone on between the two leagues would be over.

So, this representative from New York, Emmanuel Cellars, decided he wasn't going to let this happen. He was a pretty powerful guy, too. He was the chairman of the House Judiciary Committee and the Congressional Committee on Antitrust Matters. He was going to stop the merger.

Pete Rozelle called me. He was hoping I could help him talk with Joe Waggoner, who was a U.S. representative from up around Shreveport. Waggoner was on the committee, and Pete thought that Joe would help. Pete was kind of desperate to not let this merger fall apart.

I told Pete that he was going after the wrong guy. Hale Boggs was a fraternity brother of mine back at Tulane. He had more clout in Congress, and I told Pete that I thought Hale would maybe be interested in making a deal. Of course, I knew this was really our chance to get a team.

I had been working with this brilliant young man, David Kleck, a political advisor for race relations and many, many other things. So, I told Hale to meet with him, and David went up to Washington. The two of them knew exactly what to do right off. Hale attached the NFL-AFL antitrust waiver to a bill Lyndon Johnson was sure to sign. It had to do with anti-inflation measures. There was no way that Johnson was not going to sign that bill. I mean, *no way*.

Lindy Boggs

Hale knew right then that this was going to happen. Once he got the NFL business on that bill, it was no longer even a matter for Representative Cellars's committee. Russell Long now had the bill over at the Senate Finance Committee—and he was the chairman. So that wasn't going to be a problem.

Dave Dixon

It looked like a done deal, and Pete called to thank me for helping him. I said, "Well, Pete, when do we get a team, a franchise?"

"Your turn is coming," he said. "Atlanta will get a franchise, and then when we expand again, New Orleans will be right in line."

"Well," I said, "that better mean soon."

Lindy Boggs

To make sure we got the team, Hale made a point of running into Mr. Rozelle the day of the vote, right before it was about to happen. He was very clever like that.

Dave Dixon

It was actually David Kleck. He made sure that Hale and Pete would bump into each other right outside the chambers. That's no small task, you know? So the bill is just about to come to a ballot, and Rozelle figures he has what he needs. He says to Hale, "I just don't know how to thank you for what you're doing here."

"Don't know how?" Hale says, looking him right in the eye. "What do you mean you don't know how? New Orleans gets an immediate franchise in the NFL. That was our deal, right?"

Pete starts insisting that he's doing everything he can and so on and so forth. Hale looks him right in the eye, again—and you have to understand that Hale Boggs was a very powerful man at that time, one of the most powerful in Washington—he looks him in the eye and says, "Well, we can always postpone the vote while you talk to your owners." And then he turns and walks away.

At that point, Pete Rozelle knew he was licked. He could not let that merger get blocked. Can you imagine that the NFL as it is today wouldn't exist? It was a tremendous moment. So Pete races after Hale and says, "It's a deal. You'll get your franchise."

Lindy Boggs

Oh, Hale was delighted, really delighted. He was very happy that he and Senator Long had helped get this for New Orleans, and he was a very big Saints fan right away. We went to games every chance we could. We lived in Washington, and so we couldn't go too often; flying back then was not as easy as it is now. But when we did go, he would sit there and just smile. He was so proud, so proud.

Dave Dixon

I had already started work on building the Superdome. I had gone to Governor John McKeithen and told him why we needed it. He immediately saw the potential and got the ball rolling. So, we had the team, and we were going to build this incredible domed stadium right in downtown New Orleans. But we needed a place for the team to play immediately.

I was very close with the people at Tulane, and they had this tremendous stadium on campus in uptown New Orleans. Tulane played there, and of course the Sugar Bowl was there, too. I knew it was at least as good or better than a lot of the stadiums that other professional teams were using at the time.

At first the people at Tulane weren't sure if they wanted the NFL to play there, but they pretty quickly agreed that it was a good thing. So we had a place to play.

Ken Trahan, *manager, Saints Hall of Fame*

They announced a competition to name the team, and probably half the city suggested "the Saints." I don't think there was ever really any doubt that the team was going to be called that. It just seemed natural then, and I really can't imagine them being called anything else.

Dave Dixon

We knew all along that the team was going to be called the Saints. "When the Saints Go Marching In" is just so closely identified with New Orleans. It seemed to fit perfectly.

I had gone to Rome and had been granted an audience with Pope Paul VI. It wasn't just me; there were quite a few people there to see him. But in my mind I was wondering if I should ask if it was okay to name a professional football team "the Saints." Well, there we were in this little amphitheater. The pope enters in this procession, and I notice a little group of French nuns. They had just taken their vows the night before; they were all just teenagers. The monsignor explained to me that they were all going to Brazil the next day to be missionaries.

As the pope walked past them, they were so excited they could hardly contain themselves. They began to serenade him in French. I knew a little French and, of course, picked up the melody of what they were singing. I said, "My God, that's 'When the Saints Go Marching In'!!" I thought that was certainly a good sign.

I turned to the monsignor and said, "That song originated in New Orleans."

He smiled and said, "No, it was a French hymn that originated in the sixteenth century."

Either way, I thought it was a good sign. When I got back to

New Orleans, I checked it out with a jazz historian I knew, and he said, "Yes, it has been around for a very long time. We knew it was from at least the seventeenth century, but if the monsignor says it's from the sixteenth, that's good enough for us."

Lindy Boggs

With Louisiana's strong French heritage, the fleur-de-lis was perfect for the Saints' emblem. I really liked it. It wasn't just some animal on a uniform; it was a symbol of our heritage.

Ken Trahan

The fleur-de-lis is without a doubt the most unique insignia or logo in all of professional sports.

Dave Dixon

So by that point it was all settled. We'd have the fleur-de-lis on the helmets, and the team was going to be called the Saints. The name had not been announced publicly yet, but it was decided. Then John Mecom, the original owner, got cold feet about it and sent his PR guys to come see me, and we all went to lunch. Mecom wanted to talk about using a different name, because he thought it might be sacrilegious. And, at that very moment, Archbishop Philip Hannan, the brand-new archbishop of New Orleans, happened to be in the restaurant and happened to walk by our table.

I stopped him and told him about the conversation we were having, about whether or not naming the team was sacrilegious or not. "I think the Saints is a marvelous name," he said. "And besides, I have a terrible premonition that we are going to need all the help we can get."

Ken Trahan

I was at the very first game they played at Tulane Stadium. I had seats with my dad in the south end zone. It was great, just really exciting. They won a good many preseason games their first year, and then the season opener was just wild.

Tulane Stadium could hold about 80,000 people, and there wasn't an empty seat in the place. I remember this really big guy playing the trumpet in the middle of the field and wondering what the heck he was doing playing the trumpet at a football game. My dad had to explain that the man was Al Hirt and that he was one of the greatest trumpet players ever.

It was finally real, the team, the city coming together. It was just one of those magical days. The Saints were playing the Rams. On the kickoff, the Saints were going to receive. The Rams kicked off, and John Gilliam took the kick and ran 94 yards for a touchdown. The place went bananas! I thought, well, this is going to be easy.

Of course, it wasn't. The Saints lost that game—and a lot more after that one.

DO YOU KNOW WHAT IT MEANS
TO MISS NEW ORLEANS?

THEY SAY EVERY city gets the football team it deserves. For the next forty years the lovable losers known as the New Orleans Saints endured incredible mishaps, bad choices, bad drafts, and mismanagement. They lost games—a lot of them. Across all those decades, the team won only one play-off game. In fact, it was not until the strike-shortened 1987 season that they even realized a winning record. (And even then they needed Pope John Paul II to say Mass in the dome to get the right mojo.) But win or lose, the city and the team had been the ultimate playmates, and had always let the good times roll.

For team and city alike, those good times came to screeching halt when Hurricane Katrina rolled ashore. Devastated and demoralized, the city looked to its old friend for help, and, like an old friend, the Saints responded. There had always been a great love between New Orleans and her beloved Saints, and it has been said that distance makes the heart grow fonder. For now, there would be a great distance between the two. And, in the end, they did grow fonder, their bond deeper and stronger than ever before.

Mickey Loomis, *general manager, New Orleans Saints*

There wasn't any real consideration to canceling the Saints 2005 season. I know some people were speculating that it might happen, but it just wasn't. In a perfect world probably the best thing might have been to suspend our operations and let people take care of their personal issues. But you can't do that, because if one team stops their operation, then it affects the whole league and the whole schedule for every other team.

We knew that we could find a place to practice, although things would not be perfect. We could find a place to play, and we could draw fans. We could continue as a team. And we knew early on that, you know, the Saints needed to play because it gives the people of New Orleans and the people of the region something to hang on to. It's something from home even if you don't have a home.

We had to keep playing and continuing on. It's like that old saying, "No matter how hard it is, the best thing you can do is keep pushing on." Just playing, just being, just continuing to exist as the New Orleans Saints was going to be important to the psyche of our region. Even though we were in San Antonio, we remained the *New Orleans* Saints. In contrast, when the Hornets relocated to Oklahoma City, they didn't really do that.

Michael Lewis, *kick return specialist, New Orleans Saints*

Seeing what had gone on in New Orleans did hurt me a lot. I'm from New Orleans, and I saw a lot of the stuff that had happened. It looked like a ghost town when I went back to get my vehicle.

Any other season we would have been at home getting ready for the season. That's not an excuse or anything. Our job was to focus on football. Everybody was talking, and we knew what we had to do. We knew that we had to practice. We had to focus on what was at hand and get ready for Carolina.

Aaron Brooks, *quarterback, 2005 New Orleans Saints*

We knew that our fans needed us, but we needed them, too. We needed them to be strong. We wanted them to know that everything was going to be all right. We needed each other, because our main goal was to get back together in the Superdome.

Steve Gleason, *safety, New Orleans Saints*

Mr. Benson did everything he could do to make us as comfortable as we could be under the circumstances. We were living in hotels. The facilities were far from ideal, but I knew how much better we had it than a lot of people back in New Orleans. We had hot meals and water and electricity. Every day we could see on TV that people back there didn't even have those basic things.

Mickey Loomis

One thing that Mr. Benson did was to make sure that everybody who worked for us in New Orleans had the opportunity to come to San Antonio and continue to work and to continue to get a check. And he paid for a large portion of their rental costs. We were in a hotel for the first month, and he paid for that and fed everybody. He was really generous in terms of taking care of people financially.

Joe Horn, *wide receiver, New Orleans Saints*

We were living in a hotel at the time. The Marriott on Pecos, that's the name of the hotel down in San Antonio. We did what we had to do to get by and to try to be able to play football and practice and everything that's required of us as professional football players. Mr. Benson was doing all that he could so we would have some place to stay in the hotel until we could find something more long-term, be it a house or an apartment. He brought in people to help us find homes and things like that. He did a great job.

It was just mind-boggling. There were just so many distractions in San Antonio. It was hard to gather your thoughts and to think about football after you get twenty or thirty voicemail messages a day. Players were being asked for help. There were people who'd been affected by Katrina in San Antonio. They were coming by the hotel and looking for help. It's not that we didn't want to help them; we did. We all did. But we also needed some time to get ready to play football. We had to get ready to play the Panthers, and I didn't expect them to feel sorry for us. They were not going to go easy on us because we lost our home stadium. And in pro football, if you get distracted, if you don't get your mind and body right for a game, you can get seriously hurt.

Kenny Wilkerson, *sideline reporter, WWL Radio*

The station called and said that they wanted us to do the game at Carolina. Of course, Hokie Gajan who does the color commentary and I were both in New Orleans, and there were no flights going out of New Orleans yet. The team was over in San Antonio so we couldn't fly with them either. I went to the station, we picked up some equipment, and we drove to Charlotte to do the game.

I had not been doing my show because they were doing nonstop

Katrina information and talk. You know, people were still just trying to find out what was going on and where to get what they needed. Getting that information out was the main objective of the station at the time. That said, I really think that people needed a break and a distraction, so doing the game was important, too. Remember, the power was still out in a lot of places, and so was the cable. I think FOX 8 might have still been down, too. But people had radios, so they could at least listen to the game.

In what looked to be the beginning of a storybook season of its own, 2005 got off to an unlikely start. The Saints won their season opener against the Carolina Panthers in a thriller, 23–20. John Carney's 47-yard field goal in the final seconds of the game was the perfect ending for what had been an emotional trip. The night before, the team had been read a letter from New Orleans Mayor Ray Nagin, and just prior to the game, the Carolina home crowd of over 72,000 had welcomed the Saints with a standing ovation.

Jim Haslett, *head coach, 2005 New Orleans Saints*

We awarded two game balls after the game. We gave one to Mayor Ray Nagin and the city of New Orleans. The other one went into the team's trophy case.

John Carney, *field goal kicker, New Orleans Saints*

We knew what the game represented. When the game started, the players had their mind on football and on what they had to do to get the job done. I was thinking about placekicking and doing the best job that I could. Then when the buzzer went off and the game was over, I think I realized what the game meant to a lot of people.

Pam Randazza, *owner, Black & Gold Sports Shop*

Winning that first game against the Panthers, well, that was a big morale booster for everybody. We were all still shell-shocked over Katrina. The newspapers were just giving more bad news on top of more bad news, but here they'd won this game. I think everybody needed that little boost right then, a little something to be happy about for a while.

Michelle Babineaux, *owner, Michaul's Cajun Dance Hall*

My house was still there, but it had taken twenty-two feet of water. Everything inside was ruined or lost. Michaul's, my business, I had closed it for the hurricane. I thought I'd come right back and open it up again. It wasn't really damaged or anything; it was on high ground downtown, but all my business canceled.

I had us booked months in advance. I would go to the convention planners and get big groups booked. But within two days of Katrina I had people calling me, asking for their deposits back. I had no home, and I had all these people not just canceling on me but asking for their deposits back as well. I mean, I can't blame them, but it really got me depressed.

Abbe Garfinkel, *fan*

It was very hard to get news about the area where I lived, but finally they opened the parish for people to come back. When I got to my address, I could not see my house from the street through the trees and the debris. There were forty-foot trees in my yard that didn't even come from my property; they had washed up into my yard. I had to clamber and climb up over all of the debris to get up to the house—and then it was just awful, such a mess. My house is historic, it was built in the 1830s, and it sat up on these brick piers. Well, the storm surge from Lake Pontchartrain had come up and just wiped out those piers. The floor had been knocked out, and the inside was a total disaster.

We did have some luck. There was a crew on the corner down the street that was cutting limbs and trees. A friend went down and asked them if they could help us, and they literally cut a swath from the street to the house so that we could get in and out.

Mickey Loomis

We didn't want to go. We knew we could play at the Alamodome, and that we could sell tickets there, but our goal was always to get back to New Orleans as soon as possible. I think that there is a great deal of confusion and some misperceptions about that. Some of the media were saying that the move to San Antonio was permanent. That simply wasn't the case. There were the obvious concerns about when the Superdome could be opened again or, at that point, if it even *could* reopen. Remember, we're talking about a time when the damage at the Superdome hadn't even been assessed yet.

One thing that we really did not want to do, and we really were almost forced to do, was to play games in Baton Rouge. We really didn't feel that it was a good idea for the football team, for the players. We understood why some people thought it was necessary, but in retrospect it wasn't good for the team. I don't think it was really good for anybody.

Jim Haslett

I had just heard that we were going to play four games in Baton Rouge and three in San Antonio with our first one up in New York against the Giants. My job was to get them ready to play wherever they were going to play. It might have been nice to have played them all in San Antonio because people had their families there and less travel is always better for a team.

Anthony Canatella, *deputy superintendent, New Orleans Police Department*

I'll be perfectly honest with you. After being on the ground for the whole Katrina ordeal, seeing what went on in and around the dome and all across the city, I was skeptical. I didn't think they could possibly get it open again for at least five years, and by then the team would have been gone. And if that had been the case, if the Saints had left, they would not have needed the Superdome anymore. So I honestly felt that the Saints were gone, and the Superdome would be, too.

Daniel Garroway, *fan, twelve years old*

I was really worried that they might move away and not come back ever. A lot of people were saying that might happen, but I kept saying, "No, they can't leave. They have to come back." I'd have been very unhappy if they had not come back. It wouldn't be New Orleans without the Saints.

The first-week win against Carolina would prove to be the season's brightest moment. For their part in the NFL's Recover and Rebuild Hurricane Relief Weekend, the Saints faced off against the New York Giants. Although the game and its related activities helped raise money and awareness to help Gulf Coast residents, it did little to raise their spirits. The Saints lost the game 27–10. As distractions mounted and fatigue set in, the Saints would lose all but two of the remaining games on their schedule. They beat the Bills 19–7 for their only win in San Antonio.

In their other Alamodome outings they fell to the Falcons 34–31 and lost to the Lions 13–12.

Closer to home, the Saints were unable to provide fans with a single win in Baton Rouge. In their first return to Louisiana, they fell to the Dolphins, 21–6, then were beaten by the Bears, 20–17, topped by Tampa Bay, 10–3, and canned by Carolina, 27–10.

"On the road," the Saints lost to the Vikings, 33–16, and were sent packing by Green Bay, 52–3. In St. Louis, they got rammed, 28–17. They also lost at New England, 24–17, and in Atlanta, 36–17. Two-thousand-six got off to an inauspicious start with a New Year's Day loss at Tampa Bay, 27–13, to close out the schedule.

Adding injury to insult, during the week-five blowout loss at Green Bay, ace running back Deuce McAllister suffered a torn anterior cruciate ligament in his right knee. The workhorse of the Saints offense was lost for the remainder of the season. Like his team and the region, McAllister would now begin his own recovery and rebuilding and his future was just as uncertain.

As the 2005 season drew to a close, the entire Saints organization—players, coaches, and staff—were recognized with the NFL's Ed Block Courage Award. The honor is typically bestowed by teammates on a player from each of the thirty-two teams who best exemplifies the principles of sportsmanship and courage in the face of adversity. This year the club decided that every employee of the Saints organization fit that description.

Joe Horn

I don't think any team could have done any better under those circumstances, what we had to deal with in 2005. Mr. Benson did everything in his power to make things as good as he could make them, but it was just not the kind of environment where we could really get things together like we needed to, from the team point of view. The conditions there were just not good, you know?

Steve Gleason

I think we all did the best we could, but it was crazy there. We were sharing a facility with a high school team, and they had priority over us for a lot of things. We were professional football players—the NFL—and we were second to a high school team for the use of some things.

The locker room area that we used was so far from the practice fields that some guys would drive to it. We had to do walk-through practices in a parking lot once—in a parking lot. I think the worst was being told we couldn't use the Alamodome once because they had a volleyball tournament scheduled there. Can you believe it? A volleyball tournament. Please. I have nothing against volleyball. I'm just pointing to that as an example of how different it was from what we were used to. There are certain things that we need as professional athletes in order to play our best. Those things were just not there to be found.

Mickey Loomis

That season was a grind for everyone involved. You're trying to do your job to the best of your ability, and yet, at the same time, you've got all of these personal issues. And not just your own personal issues, but also the personal issues of your peers, your coworkers, your friends. And there was also tremendous uncertainty. You know, what's going to happen in three months? What's going to happen a year from now? All those things, they weigh on you.

Take the insurance issues, for example. They are hard enough for you when you're right there, but we were in San Antonio and we had our people trying to take care of their insurance issues that needed attention back in New Orleans. It was a combination of all those things. You just feel like you're grinding and grinding and not getting anywhere in a lot of ways.

The place where I was living flooded. We left on August 29th, and I didn't see it again until January 17th. You try to just put that stuff aside as best you can, but some people can't.

Joe Horn

I don't think one coach in this league would have had a winning season with that going on. I don't know how Coach Haslett made it through half of the season. I'm being honest with you, man. I don't see how he did it, but he did. He tried his best to keep all of us working as a team.

Unless you went through this as a Saints football player, unless you was there, you don't know. I hear people saying, "I understand how they feel. I feel their pain." No you don't, not unless you was there and you were on that football staff and you had to go through the hell we went through. Yes we all had money. And yes, we'd been blessed to have finances. But going through that and trying to be a professional and trying to play football?

Mickey Loomis

If you ask me if I think Tom Benson got a bad rap over setting up shop in San Antonio, I'd say without question that he has. I don't think it; I know it. A lot of big companies that had been in New Orleans moved out right after the hurricane, or are just never coming back. We were coming back. All Benson did was answer a question exactly like it should have been answered. In September, right after the storm, they asked him if he was coming back and why wouldn't he commit to coming back to New Orleans? Well, no one at that time knew if New Orleans was even going to be a viable city next month or even by next year. So, he said, "Hey, I don't know. Let's find out."

Then, as things started to get better, he committed and we came back. But, like I said, we were always the New Orleans Saints.

5

THE SUPERDOME

IN THE DAYS immediately after Hurricane Katrina, the devastation that the storm had wrought on the city stretched on for miles and miles. In the center of that, both physically and symbolically, the Superdome quickly became a lightning rod. As the long and desperate hours of Katrina grew into longer and more desperate days, it came to epitomize all the human suffering in the city.

Once upon a time, the Superdome represented all that was right in New Orleans. It was a testament to big dreams and big determination. For decades, it was the single largest domed structure in the world. Initially, it was so large that many engineers believed it impossible to erect.

In the end, the dome was not only built it also became an engine that drove New Orleans's economy. It became a catalyst, bringing about some of the city's brightest and most celebrated moments. It has hosted more Super Bowls than any other stadium in the country. It is home to the Sugar Bowl and has hosted NCAA Championships. Muhammad Ali defeated Leon Spinks there, cementing his legend as the Greatest of All Time. The largest indoor crowd ever assembled for a musical event gathered there when almost 90,000 fans rocked out to the Rolling Stones. It was where Pope John Paul II said Mass, and where George H. W. Bush accepted the Republican nomination for president of the United States in 1988.

Now, in the city's darkest hours, the Superdome represented everything that was wrong in New Orleans. Stranded citizens became news fodder, highlighting the staggering failures of the city's evacuation plan. The once gleaming white roof of the building was tattered and torn, turning an ugly shade of brown. Rain poured in through gaping holes. Contaminated floodwater inundated much of the arena's lower level. Little if anything functioned inside. The plumbing and electrical systems had failed. The sewerage system had backed up. And, without air-conditioning, the oppressive August heat raised temperatures inside the facility well north of 100 degrees.

Over 10,000 people went to the Superdome as a refuge of last resort, and there they stayed while awaiting help from the government. Sitting in the same seats they once occupied while cheering on the Saints or enjoying a concert, they suffered. Water was in short supply. Bathrooms were inoperable. The living conditions—if they could be called that—were subhuman.

Eventually, all of the refugees were evacuated to places better able to care for their needs, and the dome itself sat in woeful disrepair. Many thought it should be torn down, if for no other reason than to erase the horrible memories of what had transpired there.

But New Orleans would not be New Orleans without the Superdome. More important, as the NFL leadership made abundantly clear, New Orleans would not keep their franchise if that franchise had no place to play. After sustaining untold millions in damages, the dome needed to be rebuilt, and fast.

Doug Thornton, *general manager, Superdome*

I lived there. I'm the only person who lived through it all. I stayed in the Superdome from August 28th, the day before the storm hit, until everyone had been evacuated, five days later. I slept right here on the floor of my office. When I left, I was wearing the very same clothes I had on when I got here: the same clothes, underwear, jeans, everything, for five days. My toilet didn't work, either.

I saw suffering that I can't describe to you. We did what we could with what we had, but we were not set up as a shelter. We really had nothing to give people but a roof over their heads. The only goal of opening the Superdome before Katrina was to save people from the storm. We did that. The Superdome saved lives. I think if it had not been here, a lot of these people would have died. Realistically, you could say that six or seven thousand more people would have died.

Mitch Landrieu, *lieutenant governor, Louisiana*

As soon as the hurricane passed, we began surveying the damage. Tourism is our state's second-biggest industry. That's a lot of jobs, a lot of people. I knew, we all knew, that we had to see what was left of the infrastructure of that industry.

The Superdome and the Convention Center are obviously the two main venues that allow us to attract the conventions and the sports and entertainment events that support the economy. It's not just about the Saints. The Superdome brings in a lot of other people for the Sugar Bowl, Tulane football, the Essence Festival, and so many other things. It was vital that we find out immediately if it could ever reopen. We needed the Superdome not just as a venue but for the jobs it creates. I had seen the dome from the outside, and I knew that it was badly damaged. We just needed to see *how* badly damaged. Could it be saved?

Dave Dixon, *"Father of the Superdome"*

When I saw the images on television, I just couldn't believe what I was seeing. And they kept showing the Superdome. What I knew, and maybe not many people knew, was that the actual structure of the Superdome was fine. When we designed it, it was built in such a way that the building itself could withstand winds of over 300 miles per hour. So I knew it was okay from a structural standpoint. It had held up just like we predicted all those years ago. Those guys did one heck of a job designing that place. They even tested it in wind tunnels. It really is a marvel of engineering.

Mickey Loomis, *general manager, New Orleans Saints*

Personally, I had never been through a hurricane, so I had no idea, visually, of what kind of damage one could do. Seeing the Superdome like that caught me off guard. We had just played there that Friday night. The whole situation didn't seem real. The homes destroyed and people losing everything they had, it was just horrifying. I saw all of that damage and thought, what is going to happen to these people? What is going to happen to New Orleans?

The media kept showing the Superdome and everything that was going on there. It was something I just don't think anyone could be prepared for. I live in New Orleans. I have a house there. Like everybody, I was concerned about my family and my house. But I was worried about the dome, too. I knew how many people depended on it. Pretty soon I wondered, "Were we going back to the Superdome this season? Can it be fixed?" And honestly, I didn't know if anybody would ever want to go back inside.

Doug Thornton

After five days of living in that hell, I got out of there. The National Guard got me out. I went to my neighborhood, to my house. It was worse than I could have imagined. My wife got me some clothes, and I knew I had to go right back to the dome. We had to get to work. It seems like I was hardly gone when I had to go back. I knew this building as well or better than anybody. I knew it could be rebuilt. I knew it had to be rebuilt.

After a disaster like this, FEMA calls a lot of the shots, especially for a building like the Superdome. If it had been damaged more than 50%, FEMA would have insisted it be torn down. It would have had to be imploded, and it would have taken no less than thirty-six months, at best, to build a new stadium. If there were no stadium, no Superdome for the Saints to play in, the city was going to lose the team. It was just that simple: No dome, no Saints.

Mitch Landrieu

What people may not realize is that the Superdome was well insured. I mean, really well insured. We were concerned that FEMA might insist that it be torn down. I felt that if the stadium could be rebuilt, we were going to be able to rebuild it with that insurance money and other sources of funds.

And, you know, Tom Benson had been talking about a new stadium. So there were a lot of factors that came into play here. Like everything after Katrina, time was critical. Whatever we were going to do, we had to decide quickly. We had to do it right.

Doug Thornton

Governor Kathleen Blanco—and I give her a lot of credit—asked me, "Can it be done?"

I hesitated for a second, and then I said, "Yes. Yes, the Superdome can be reopened."

She said, "Then let's make it happen."

She told me to tell her what I needed, and she would make sure we cut through the red tape so we could get our job done.

The NFL was, of course, very concerned. Any thoughts about the Saints coming back during the '05 season were long gone. They wanted to know what the situation down here was.

Paul Tagliabue came down, and he immediately put me at ease. I had been dealing with politicians and local and federal leaders almost nonstop since the hurricane. I had been going 24/7. Keep in mind that my home was in ruins. I was trying to put the Superdome back together and at the same time get my own life back to something near normal.

Paul—and I will never forget this—came through the door and looked me right in the eye and asked, "How are *you?*"

He didn't ask about the dome or the economy. He asked about me. I had many great dealings with him in the past, and I knew that this was the kind of man he was. I knew that he would look at this from more than a league and business point of view. He was also looking at it from a human point of view.

We had a meeting that included Paul and other key NFL people, as well as Mr. Benson. From the start of the meeting, Paul set a tone: if the Superdome could be reopened, the Saints were staying. He made sure we all knew that the NFL was going to do everything it could to help the city get back on track. All he really wanted to know was how soon we could get the dome back open, and what could he do to help?

Of course, Mr. Benson had concerns both logistically and financially, but he and Paul Tagilabue agreed that it was the right thing to do.

Mitch Landrieu

We had the money from insurance to cover most of the damage to the Superdome; FEMA would cover much of the rest. Now we just had to get the right people in here and get it done. I knew Doug Thornton was the right man to see this through.

A lot of people asked, "How can you spend tens of millions of dollars on a stadium when people don't have homes to go back to?" The first answer is that this was insurance money; it could really only be spent rebuilding the dome. And, yes, we were going to get FEMA money to help in the effort. But—and this is hard to explain sometimes—this money comes from an entirely different budget. We were not using money that in any way could have gone to rebuilding homes or schools or anything like that.

And the second response—and it is why I have the job I have; it's what my office does—was that we had to do it to kick-start the economy. Rebuilding the Superdome would immediately create construction jobs, and it would eventually give us back the jobs that were related to the Superdome before the hurricane. Let's face it. We needed to get our people back to work. The Superdome would do that.

Doug Thornton

I think we all knew that not rebuilding the dome would be a huge psychological blow to the city. It would have taken a while to tear it down, so it would have sat right there in downtown New Orleans, abandoned and in ruins. You can see the Superdome from almost every direction when you come into the city. What do you think it would have done to the heart of the people if it had just sat here, rotting? And then, if it did come down, what would be here? For a long time there'd be nothing: just a big, gaping hole in the middle of the city.

Even the announcement that the Superdome would be rebuilt lifted people's spirits. We hired a lot of people here. We're talking about almost $200 million of work. We had contractors, subcontractors. I'd like to say, too, that these guys who came to work here took incredible pride in their jobs. Every single one of them knew how important this place was to the city. I can't tell you how many times I wound up talking to a worker, and he'd tell me about games or events he had been to here. The dome meant something to these guys on a personal level. It meant a lot to them that they were physically taking part in rebuilding their city. They worked really long hours and did a great job—a fantastic job.

Dave Dixon

I knew that the Superdome could be rebuilt. I knew Doug Thornton pretty well, and I don't know if there was a man on this planet better suited to the task of getting that job done than him. If he had told Governor Blanco or Paul Tagliabue or anybody else that the Superdome could not be rebuilt, if he had even told them that he was not going to lead the effort, then, *poof!* I doubt it would have been attempted. There was nobody else here who could have gotten that job done.

Doug Thornton

We were really steaming along with the renovations when I got a call from NFL chief operating officer Roger Goodell. This was in

December of '05. The plan had been to have the Superdome ready for December of '06, a full year from then. And you have to understand that that was quite a task. I felt certain that we could meet that goal.

So, Roger asks me, "When will the dome be ready?"

I assured him that we would be fully "football ready" on schedule, which was next December. Then he asked—I'll never forget this—he asked, "Could we maybe make it September?"

He told me that if we had turf on the floor and lights in the rafters, and I could assure him that it was safe, he could assure me that the Saints would be back playing in the fall. They would be back in the Superdome, back in New Orleans.

I told him how much more that would cost, and that we really did not have the budget for that kind of schedule. I mean, we're talking millions and millions.

"So," he asked, "it can be done if you have the money?"

"Yes."

"Then do it. The Saints will be there in the fall."

Mickey Loomis

Once we knew that we could return to New Orleans, all of our attention was focused not just on going back but on giving those fans a quality football team. We knew we had to meet the challenge. I knew, Tom knew, that just being back was not going to be enough. The whole organization felt that we had to be better. New Orleans and the Mississippi Coast were rebuilding. The Superdome was rebuilding. We knew that the Saints had to rebuild too.

6

KICKING IT UP A NOTCH

PERHAPS THE GREATEST thing that can be said about the 2005 Saints is that they finished the year out. Just making it through that hard slog of homelessness, misery, and doubt was a triumph in and of itself. How good would the team have been if not for Hurricane Katrina? That question will always linger, but sports is about what goes into the record books, and rightly so. New Orleans finished the season 3–13.

As the city worked toward its newly restored stadium, they needed a newly restored team to play in it. The first step in that rebuilding process was the hiring of Sean Payton, the team's fourteenth head coach in its forty-year history. At the time, Payton was serving as the assistant head coach for the Dallas Cowboys under Bill Parcells. And when Saints General Manager Mickey Loomis began courting him, Payton was no stranger to NFL head-coaching offers; he had already declined a previous offer to lead the Oakland Raiders.

In his previous coaching gigs, Sean Payton's talents were always perfectly suited to maximize the potential of his quarterbacks. In 2000, as the offensive co-ordinator for the New York Giants, he helped them capture the NFC title and a berth in Super Bowl XXXV. Since that year, no quarterback coached by him had thrown for less than 3,000 yards in a season. And so, when addressing the team's pressing need at quarterback, it is no wonder that Payton was able to attract free agency's most highly prized player, former Purdue Boilermaker Drew Brees. Although Brees had suffered a late-season shoulder injury, many teams in the NFL expected to vie for his services.

Brees had spent the past five seasons as a San Diego Charger, with four of those as their starter. During that time, he had thrown for over 12,000 yards, completing 1,125 of 1,809 passes. His 80 touchdowns against only 53 interceptions proved his worth, as did his leading the Chargers to the AFC West title and his 2004 trip to the Pro Bowl.

The Saints and their new head coach knew that a player like Drew Brees, coupled with other talented players, would immediately begin the rebuilding process the team sorely needed.

Mickey Loomis, *general manager, New Orleans Saints*

At the end of the '05 season, we needed to look toward the future, and we decided to make the coaching change. You know, I looked at the team, and here we were in this deep hole, this abyss. We were 3–13, and then on top of that you had all this uncertainty about the city. So many questions: Where would we be playing? Where would we be practicing? Where would our players and our coaches and our staff people live? The last season had been such a grind that I knew we had to get somebody in here with a lot of energy.

We needed somebody who could do two things. One, lift up and inspire the organization; two, at the same time, give us a good kick in the ass, because we were going to need that. We were going to need somebody with charisma, but who also could impart some discipline, some toughness.

So generally—not always, but generally—that's going to take a younger guy; a guy who is looking to make his mark, as opposed to somebody who has already made his mark and is just looking to continue with that. In fact, we interviewed two guys who had been head coaches. We met with Mike Martz and Mark Sherman. They both are great coaches and could have been great choices for the Saints, just maybe under different circumstances.

We also needed a guy with connections, so he could attract good assistant coaches to work with him. He needed to be able to bring in free agents out on the market who would get excited about playing for him. We couldn't really sell free agents on the city yet, and we couldn't sell them on the team, because we had just finished a 3–13 season. So what we were going to be selling these guys was a new head coach.

One of the advantages of being in pro football today is that, at some point in their career, most players do have a chance to decide where they want to play. That choice comes down to a lot of different things, and it depends a lot on timing. It may come down to wanting to play in the area where they grew up or where they played college ball. It may come down to, "Hey, I want to play for this particular organization." Many times it comes down to, "I want to play for *this guy*." And we felt that Sean Payton was that type of guy. Players would want to play for him, and that is where you begin to build a team. We were looking at a tremendous challenge, and Sean Payton was the right man to tackle that challenge.

Sean Payton, *head coach, New Orleans Saints*

I was excited about talking with the Saints. I knew that they had not been a very successful franchise over the years, but I had heard about the fans. Of course, I had been there many times and knew a bit about the culture and had enjoyed the food and the music. Who doesn't, right?

When I told Bill Parcells in Dallas that I was thinking about taking the Saints job, he told me to see if I could figure out why they had not done well over the years. Identify what the problem is, and then see if I could avoid it.

I knew that there were a lot of distractions here, and that we'd have to get players with real character to play here, to win here and not get distracted. I felt that the organization was committed to bringing in that type of player.

I was concerned about whether or not the Superdome would be ready or not; you know, that the Saints would really be back in New Orleans full time. I was really pleased and excited that they had a great practice facility that was state of the art and 100% functioning. So I knew that at least that part of the equation had been answered.

Throughout the process it was clear that Mr. Benson, Mickey Loomis, and his staff were doing everything they could, under difficult circumstances, to bring in a coach. They wanted to create an environment to make this city and this area proud.

On January 19, 2006, Mickey Loomis and Tom Benson introduced Sean Payton as the new head coach of the New Orleans Saints.

Mickey Loomis

We really didn't hold anything back. We made sure he knew what he was in for, and Sean responded to it. He's the type of guy who likes a challenge. We knew he could do it for us. When he said he would, I knew we were off and running.

You never really know for sure about these things, but I felt very good about Sean Payton being the head coach of the New Orleans Saints. John Fox told me personally that Sean has the "it" factor, and

I agree with him. I think we hired a coach who has what it takes to finally bring a championship to this city. And this is a city that is very deserving of a championship.

Tom Benson, *owner, New Orleans Saints*

We were starting a new chapter in the history of our team, and as we moved forward, we were going to face many new challenges. I was proud of the choice that Mickey made in Sean. As you looked at what he had done already in his short career it's really very impressive, very outstanding. I was very excited about what our future held.

Sean Payton

I believe in the process. I believe in preparation. I believe in attention to detail. There is nothing magical about winning in this league. It's the same with every winning team: preparation and attention to detail.

In the NFL, there really is no downtime. As soon as I got to New Orleans, we went to work, assessing the players we had and looking at the free agency market. We all agreed that we would look for and do our best to get tough, disciplined, smart football players. Those are the players you win football games with.

I knew that Deuce McAllister had suffered a serious knee injury. I knew he was coming along but wasn't sure if we were going to be looking for a running back. There was obviously a need at quarterback. And there are only two ways to get one: free agency or the draft.

Mickey Loomis

In our minds, Drew Brees was the best free agent on the market. He was the best player available, period. Just to get him to come visit and kick the tires in New Orleans was an important message to all of the free agents and their agents. It said, "You know what? *New Orleans is still viable.* They've got a lot of uncertainty. They got a new head coach, and they are coming off of a 3–13 season, but they are still an NFL team and a very viable option."

Sean Payton

Drew is a great guy. He's smart, and he has been a winner everywhere he has ever been. He is the kind of guy that you want on your team. He can make a team better immediately. We're kind of in the talent-acquisition business. We identify a player that fits what we're looking for, then we want to be aggressive and get into the process of recruiting him. Getting Drew here really started that process for us. So we were very excited that he decided to visit.

Drew Brees, *quarterback, New Orleans Saints*

It was an interesting time to visit. I think the Saints—Mickey Loomis, Sean Payton, Mr. Benson, everybody—wanted to be perfectly honest with me about both the problems in New Orleans and the opportunities I could have here. They wanted to make sure that I knew that this was a place where I could live.

They showed me that there was a lot of New Orleans that was reopening and resurging, but that there was also a lot of New Orleans that needed work and needed help; there was a lot of work to be done. They let me know that I could be a large part of the rebuilding process for the team—and the city.

I am always one to try and take a negative and turn it into a positive, and I believe that everything happens for a reason. I truly believe that I was put in this position for a reason. I was thankful for being presented this opportunity. For most people, an opportunity like this one doesn't come around in their lifetime and yet it was there for me. To be a part of a turnaround within this organization but also for the city of New Orleans and this entire Gulf Coast region—I just felt like it was meant to be. It was meant to be.

Sean Payton

I was building a house on the North Shore, and I thought that while spending time with Drew and his wife, Brittany, I'd show them that area. I'd show them that there were many good options for finding a place to live. So I took them across Lake Pontchartrain and drove them around.

The plan was to bring them back to the facility and then back to their hotel to let them rest and freshen up. We had plans to eat at Emeril's later that night. Somehow—and I still don't remember where or how—I took a wrong turn. I was still new to the area, and I got lost.

Here I am driving Drew and Brittany around and trying to show him why he should play for me and the Saints, and I'm lost. It wasn't really how I had planned things out.

Mickey Loomis

Sean called me. I think he had been driving around with Drew and his wife for an hour or more not knowing where he was. He was certain that he had blown the whole deal and lost Drew.

We got him back to the practice facility and made plans for dinner at Emeril's, which, at that time, was really one of the only places open. Emeril [Lagasse] has a national reputation, which was really lucky for us. Emeril may have helped seal the deal.

Drew Brees

We got to Emeril's, and there was a book at my place at the table. It was one of his cookbooks. Emeril wasn't there, but he had put the book there. Inside there was a note: "If you sign with the Saints, I'll cook your first meal here in New Orleans at your house." That was pretty cool, because he's a legend not just down here but also throughout the country and the world. It was neat, a nice welcome to the city.

Emeril Lagasse, *chef*

Drew is a great guy. I was in New York taping my show when they held the press conference announcing he would join the Saints. Toward the end of the conference, Brees said, "Emeril, I'll take you up on that dinner."

Sean Payton

I liked Drew as a player, but I was really impressed that he was up for the challenges off the field as well. I felt we had a winner, a real class guy with a lot of character.

Mickey Loomis

I think for this team, the most important thing was signing Sean Payton as head coach. The second most important thing was signing Drew Brees. That was a huge deal for us. Not only did he commit to us as a team, but he and his wife really did commit to the city and the area. They took out a full-page ad in the paper, saying how happy they were to be in New Orleans and how they were going to jump in with both feet to be part of the community and part of the rebuilding of the city. They bought a house in the city, and they're committed to that. You really couldn't ask for a more perfect situation or response at a time when New Orleans and the Saints needed it the most.

In order to rebuild, the Saints needed more than just a new quarterback. They had many positions to upgrade, and linebacker was one of them. To bolster that part of his roster, Sean Payton looked to his previous employer, the Dallas Cowboys. Scott Fujita had played college ball at California and had been drafted in the fifth round by the Kansas City Chiefs. Joe Vitt, a Saints assistant head coach, was Fujita's coach there. And current Saints defensive coordinator Gary Gibbs had coached Fujita in Dallas, after the linebacker was acquired by the Cowboys in a trade. All around, the feelings for Fujita were good.

Sean Payton

Obviously, Gary and I were familiar with Scott Fujita from our time in Dallas. Joe Vitt knew him in Kansas City. Scott defines the type of person we're looking for: a dedicated veteran who's been a starter and knows what it takes to succeed. Scott understood the system that Gary was putting in place here, and that was an advantage for all of us. That was a real win-win situation.

Mickey Loomis

We were targeting players we believed would make an impact. We were also looking for guys with great character. Scott is a smart, athletic player and picked up our system pretty quickly. He did everything we could have asked of him.

Scott Fujita, *linebacker, New Orleans Saints*

When New Orleans called, it was a trip that both my wife and I definitely wanted to take. It was great to see a city on the mend. I just felt like there was so much upside to the organization and the city. We felt comfortable right away, and we felt great about canceling the rest of our trips. To tell you the truth, we wouldn't be here if we didn't feel that there was a tremendous upside with the new coaching staff, if I didn't believe in the organization, and if I didn't believe in the city.

7

A GOOD DAY AT THE OFFICE

THE FREE AGENCY period had brought the Saints good fortune in their quest to assemble a winning team. Now, with a 2005 record of 3–13, the Saints had the dubious honor of owning the second overall selection in the upcoming NFL Draft. It was not the first time that the Saints had held a high pick. In fact, their checkered history of losing seasons had them at the head of the pack on draft day quite frequently.

The collapse of quarterback Aaron Brooks, a player once thought to be a godsend for the team, mandated an immediate change. Signing Drew Brees had solidified that position, giving the team more flexibility when eyeing the talent coming from the college ranks.

Without a doubt, the most exciting player available in the 2006 draft—perhaps for the past few drafts—was USC running back Reggie Bush. On his way to winning the Heisman Trophy in 2005, the former Trojan had led the nation with an average of 222 total yards per game. Bush had gained 1,740 yards on the ground, running into the end zone sixteen times. He added another 478 yards and 2 touchdowns with his 37 receptions. Oh yeah, he also returned punts.

Clearly, Reggie Bush was any coach's dream. The Houston Texans, with the first overall pick, were sure to bring Reggie home. His eventual selection by the Saints at the second overall spot was a surprise, but it placed him in good company. Thirty-five years earlier, the team had selected the greatest Saint of them all, Archie Manning, at the same spot in the draft.

With Reggie Bush safely on board, other pressing needs needed to be addressed, especially on defense. With a good plan and a little good luck, many of them were. And by the end of the draft, the 2006 off-season would prove to be the most successful in franchise history.

Mickey Loomis, *general manager, New Orleans Saints*

At the end of the 2005 season, we'd thought we'd be looking for a quarterback with our pick. But with Drew coming on board, we could address some other needs.

It looked like Reggie Bush was going to be drafted by Houston, so we were looking at a number of guys—all really good, quality players that could have helped us. We had kind of prepared for the possibility that Houston might pass on Reggie, but we really didn't expect that to be the case. Reggie, at least to us, was just that special.

It seems like so many good things happen at Emeril's. We're having dinner on Friday night before the draft; I'm there with Coach Payton and all the guys from our scouting department—and all our phones start ringing simultaneously. Sean has a lot of sources in the national media, and so do I. His guys are telling him that they think Houston is now going to sign Mario Williams, the great defensive end. Meanwhile, my guys are calling me and telling me that, no, Houston has a deal done with Reggie Bush and that we would be on the clock.

Sean Payton, *head coach, New Orleans Saints*

Mickey and the scouts, they all had BlackBerrys and things like that, but I'm pretty low-tech. I just had my cell phone. My guy is pretty well connected in the media, and he's telling me that Houston is not taking Reggie, that they've made a deal with Mario Williams. My guy was positive that that was a done deal.

Mickey Loomis

We had just assumed that Houston would take Reggie, but now we had to consider the option. You know, how do we feel about Reggie given that we already have Deuce McAllister and some other good running backs? Our real need was on defense. How would we feel if Reggie Bush is available? And it was unanimous. We all said, "Look, we've got to take him. We just can't pass up this guy."

At one point, Sean said, "I'll bet you each twenty dollars that we get Reggie Bush."

So, we all bet him twenty dollars that there was no way that was going to happen.

Sean Payton

After we made the bet, I had to go to the men's room, so I got up from the table and left.

Mickey Loomis

A few minutes later, all of our phones start ringing like crazy again. This time all our sources are saying that Houston has made a commitment to Mario Williams, and that we're on the clock. If we want

Reggie Bush, we have the opportunity to take him. We all start high-fiving each other; we were all really excited.

Sean Payton

I got back to the table, and there was a stack of twenties at my place. It was great, really great. Suddenly, it seemed that the whole place knew. Even Emeril came over to the table and congratulated us.

Mickey Loomis

Immediately after dinner, we all went back to the Saints facility and sat down and started putting our options up on a board. "Okay," we said, "what happens if somebody offers us a blockbuster trade for Reggie?" You know, what would be the line of demarcation for us? What would we actually take in order to trade the pick? And I can tell you: We couldn't come up with anything.

The next day, we had a couple of offers but nothing that we really considered. So we took him, and it has proven to be a great pick for us. Reggie is a unique and special talent.

Pam Randazza, *owner, Black & Gold Sports Shop*

Things had been going so well with the team. They had gotten Sean Payton and Drew Brees and some other really good guys. The fans were really feeling good and getting excited.

Then we got Reggie Bush. Houston sure let that one slip by. Maybe it was all those prayers we had been saying. I don't know why they didn't want him, because we sure did. I got on the phone right away with my distributors. I knew without a doubt we were going to be selling *a lot* of Reggie Bush jerseys.

Reggie Bush, *running back, New Orleans Saints*

Obviously, initially, I was a little disappointed because I wanted to be the first overall pick. But you never know what's in store for you.

Sean Payton

You have to understand that Reggie had expected to be the first guy drafted. Dropping to that second slot might not seem like a big deal to most people, but it is a big deal to a guy like Reggie. He's just that determined and dedicated. He had been told for months that he was going number one.

Mickey Loomis

Maybe he wasn't the first pick in the league, but he was always the guy we considered the best player in the draft. He would have been our pick if we had been picking first.

So, yeah, he kind of had the rug pulled out from under him. He was all set to go to Houston, this big, thriving city with a new team and a great, brand-new stadium. Now, all of a sudden, he's coming to New Orleans. The city's in disarray, nobody's certain what's going to happen, and we're a team that's just gone 3–13. But you have to give this kid a lot of credit. He jumped in with both feet.

Kenny Wilkerson, *sideline reporter, WWL Radio*

I just really couldn't believe that Houston would pass on Reggie and we might get him. Even after the Mario Williams deal was announced, I thought maybe the Saints would trade the pick away. It didn't really sink in until they made the announcement. I mean, what do you say? Was it luck? Divine intervention?

There were rumors. There was some talk that maybe it was too good to be true. People were whispering that maybe somebody at the NFL had suggested that Houston not take Reggie, that they should let the Saints have him. I find that hard to believe. I think Houston just decided to pass. All that I know—and all that really matters—is that we got him.

Drew Brees, *quarterback, New Orleans Saints*

I honestly didn't think we'd be getting a running back in the draft. We already had Deuce, and he is a truly great player. But when I saw that we were going to get Reggie, I was really psyched.

Bobby Hebert, *former quarterback, New Orleans Saints*

You really can't have too many good players. As a quarterback, I can tell you that for sure. But with all the problems the Saints had had in the past with superstar running back Ricky Williams, I thought they might trade the pick away. When they took him, I thought, wow, this team might be *good*. Drew Brees, and now Reggie Bush? I knew Deuce's surgeon, and I knew that he was coming along well with his rehab. So I knew he'd be back, too.

So, as a quarterback, I was immediately thinking about all the things the Saints would be able to do on offense. It was going to be fun.

Joe Horn, *wide receiver, New Orleans Saints*

Reggie is a competitor and a great athlete. I knew that this was going to be very good for this team, very good. I was glad to have him.

Kenny Wilkerson

All of the calls to our show were saying that this was the biggest pick by the Saints since Archie Manning. It was just that big.

Emeril Lagasse, *chef*

Mickey Loomis and Coach Peyton were at Emeril's on a Friday. They ate and left but we didn't know what was going down. The next day they called and said, "We need a table in about four hours. We're bringing home Reggie Bush."

When Reggie walked in, the whole restaurant jumped to their feet and started chanting "Reggie! Reggie! Reggie!" He thought the Saints had set it up.

This year, for the 2007 season, they didn't want to jinx themselves, so they came back to the restaurant before the draft. We pulled the ticket from last year, and they had the same food, same seat, same table.

Mickey Loomis

We really had some things go our way that day. You have to be always looking for opportunities to get good players and be ready to jump on them. We had the thirty-fourth pick in the second round. Cleveland offered us Jeff Faine if we would take their pick, the forty-third. Jeff is a solid player at center. He had started over thirty games for the Browns since they drafted him in 2003.

Sean Payton

Jeff's a guy who has started in this league, and who was a first-round draft pick. He's a very intelligent guy, and we thought he could help us in regards to losing LeCharles Bentley. Just like we had hoped to, we were building this team up, step-by-step, rebuilding and upgrading the roster. That's our job in the off-season.

Jeff Faine, *center, New Orleans Saints*

I wasn't really concerned about looking for a job; for me it was really about a fresh start. I was excited about coming to New Orleans and being a part of the Saints—to be a part of everything that they were doing and that was taking place down here.

Mickey Loomis

We had our eye on Roman Harper for safety. He was high on our list. We needed to upgrade on defense, and we felt that Roman would be a good addition to the team. So we used our second-round pick to get him.

Sean Payton

As we began to evaluate this draft class and stack our picks and look at the board, Roman was a guy that we had rated very high. He had been a three-year starter at Alabama and had been a team captain his senior year. He has all of the things we look for in a player. We were really glad that he was available to us when we had the opportunity to take him.

Roman Harper, *safety, New Orleans Saints*

I was really surprised when my agent told me that New Orleans's general manager was on the phone. I just wasn't ready for it. It was crazy. I really hadn't been paying attention to the draft. I had been told that I'd be in the first round, maybe, or maybe the second. I really didn't know where I was going, but I was happy to be going to the Saints. They're so close to home for me. I have family in Mobile, and my brother is a big Saints fan. I said to my brother, "I hope the Saints have enough money left for me after they sign Reggie." I was really excited about playing with Reggie.

Mickey Loomis

We had a terrific first day, and the second day was pretty darn good, too. In the fourth round, we picked up Jahri Evans to help out at tackle. We had made a deal with the Eagles to swap picks, and for that we picked up defensive tackle Hollis Thomas. He's a guy we thought could have an immediate impact, and he did.

And of course, everybody knows about Marques Colston. That was really a blessing to get him there, especially that late in the last round of the draft.

Rick Mueller, *director of player personnel, New Orleans Saints*

In the draft, we tried to stick with the best player available, which we always do. We drafted Marques in the seventh round, and he was going to play wide receiver for us. He was never going to play tight end, but we got that question a lot. It's funny. That's nothing that we discussed or that even came up.

We just liked him. He's 6'4½"—and the kid could run. He was dominant at his position at Hofstra. He had great size, and when you looked at our receivers, you didn't see a lot of big guys. I don't think there was a guy over six feet among them. He brought a combination of speed and size, something that we didn't have. And we liked that.

Sean Payton

I had been through the draft as an assistant. I knew something about what it would be like, but this time around I was the head coach, the guy. Overall, I felt really good about it. Looking back, it was outstanding. I knew we had to keep building on what we had, but we had gotten a lot accomplished, both in free agency and in the draft.

Kenny Wilkerson

You had to feel good about what the Saints had gotten done in the draft. I don't want to say that they stole Reggie Bush, but it sure felt like it. And, looking back now, you have to say the same thing about Marques Colston. Who could have imagined that this guy from Hofstra—which is not really a big-time program—would turn out to be so good? He was almost an afterthought, you know, "Oh yeah, we also picked up this big kid named Colston at the end of the draft." And then he turns out to be one of the biggest stories of the year. He and Reggie both were real close to being rookie of the year. I think it's safe to say that if he had not gotten hurt and missed a few games, then he definitely would have been rookie of the year. Amazing.

Shortly after being drafted by the Saints—and even before he had signed his first professional football contract—Reggie Bush made a bold statement about his wanting to be a part of the New Orleans community. Knowing how important high school football is—not just for athletes but to the entire community—Bush paid to have the playing surface at New Orleans's historic Tad Gormley Stadium refurbished. The stadium, built during the Great Depression by the Works Progress Administration, sits in the middle of City Park and had been covered by several feet of saltwater after the levees broke. Bush Field at Tad Gormley Stadium, as it was renamed, once again plays host to dozens of gridiron matches each fall. The season had not yet begun, and the Saints were already making a difference.

FORGING A TEAM

FREE AGENCY HAD brought the team stability at several key positions, and the draft had helped with others. There were, however, huge questions hovering over the team in the months leading up to training camp. Deuce McAllister had suffered a serious knee injury. While the prognosis was good, no one could really be sure until he took hits and tested it. Similarly, the Saints had taken a tremendous gamble on Drew Brees, who had suffered an injury to his shoulder. The Saints were confident that both players' work ethic would get them through rehabilitation programs.

As the excitement of draft day faded, Sean Payton began taking steps to take a group of talented football players and turn them into a team. That year, in an effort to get the players out and away from the distractions of the city, training camp would be held at Millsaps College in Jackson, Mississippi. But first, before training camp, before the conditioning drills and the practice games could begin, there was one important thing that the team needed to do.

Will Smith, *defensive end, New Orleans Saints*

They took us paintballing. It was to help us come together as a team. We found out about it at around 7:30 a.m. We went up to Mandeville, and they had the stuff all set up for us. When we got there, we already knew which teams we were going to be on. It was a lot of guys' first time doing it. I've been paintballing before, but never on a course as big as this one. So it was a lot of fun.

Steve Gleason, *safety, New Orleans Saints*

Once we heard what we would be doing, some of us took it a little further. We really got into it. A few of us, Drew Brees , John Carney, and me, we brought along that black stuff that you use under your eyes to keep the glare out in a game. We started putting it all over our faces, camouflage-style. Man, it was awesome.

Sean Payton, *head coach, New Orleans Saints*

This was in mid-June, and we just thought we should change things up a bit, make things fun. When you change things up once in a while, there's something to be gained from it. Certainly, as a staff, we thought this was something that we needed.

Will Smith

The coaches got out there, too. Even Coach Payton.

Steve Gleason

For the last game, Coach Payton goes out there. Now, I really didn't know him all that well, what with him being new and all. I wasn't sure what he was like.

I'm sitting there behind some bushes, and here he comes. He walks right into my line of fire, and I'm thinking, do I take him out? Is he going to be cool with that? Anyway, I just fire and I nail him. I start screaming, "I got Coach Payton! I got Coach Payton!" It was really great.

Sean Payton

It was a clean shot.

Steve Gleason

What you need when you are coming together as a team is conversation. You need the guys to communicate. In sports, and especially pro sports, sometimes you're all into what you need to get done, and so you don't communicate as much as you would like.

That day, we were all talking, and we got to know each other outside of football. We started to laugh together. On the ride back, everybody was having a good time in a way that you really can't after a game or a practice. At those times, you really should be thinking about football and not laughing, but this was just the opposite. It was brilliant. We were bonding.

Sean Payton

I think it was a success. We got some really good feedback after that. I could see that we had accomplished something positive.

Mickey Loomis, *general manager, New Orleans Saints*

I felt really good about what we had done so far as an organization. We were able to attract some really good people here, and we were getting the things done that needed to be done. We had gotten some of the very best free agents available and addressed pressing needs during that period. And we'd had a heck of a draft. We got to know the new players during workouts and in the minicamps. Sean got to know and work with the veterans then also. The next task was to bring it all together.

Sean Payton

The off-season had been outstanding from the standpoint of getting the guys in condition with running and lifting weights. Certainly they were in better shape than they had been at the first minicamp we had with them just before the draft. It was going pretty smoothly.

Kenny Wilkerson, *sideline reporter, WWL Radio*

You really didn't know what to expect at training camp that year. Drew Brees had all the makings of a good quarterback and seemed like a great guy, but you still had to ask yourself, "Why had the Chargers been willing to let him go?" And there really were huge, gaping holes in the defense.

A big question was, "When will Reggie Bush get to camp? Will he hold out? How soon can they get everybody here?"

Mickey Loomis, *general manager, New Orleans Saints*

It's a priority to get these young players signed and into camp. That was a major priority for us. These negotiations take time and attention to detail and a lot of work. Russ Ball, our vice president of football administration, was a key factor in getting a lot of that done. His efforts got a lot of our key guys here for the start of camp.

Kenny Wilkerson

Reggie signed his deal with the Saints on or around August 1st. I think the deal had really been worked out before then, but it took him forever to get to Jackson to actually sign and report. I think it took him literally a whole day to get to Jackson from Los Angeles, but he was in camp.

Bobby Hebert, *former quarterback, New Orleans Saints*

I can't tell you how important it is to have all the time you can in training camp to work with your guys. As a quarterback you have to know how guys run their routes. They have to get used to how you throw and that kind of thing. That takes time and reps. You have to find the rhythms and get the timing down.

The offensive line has to get used to playing as a unit, too, and the defense has to be playing together. So you really need everybody to be in camp healthy and on time. My hat is really off to these guys that they got all that done the way that they did. Having your number one pick in camp that early was big for the team, but also for Reggie.

Reggie Bush, *running back, New Orleans Saints*

It was time to go to work.

Sean Payton

It meant a lot to have Reggie there and ready to go. His people worked hard to get him here and he showed up ready to work. We got him started in the meetings and then into the practice routines. It was exciting to have all of our players here.

Mickey Loomis

Suddenly, with Reggie here, we were overloaded at the running back position. We already had Deuce and felt positive that he would be just fine. We also had Aaron Stecker. We had signed Michael Bennett in March and so we could trade him. We made a deal with Kansas City. Michael was a consummate pro in the prime of his career, and he would be a good addition to any team. He deserved an opportunity to play, so we felt the trade was good for us and for him.

Sean Payton

The thing about Michael—and it's unique in this day and age—is that his approach in the off-season was just unbelievable. He had trained hard. He had prepared hard. I appreciated that, and I think he knew that. I'd have liked to have him on the team, but it really would not have been fair, to him. I told him, "You are going to be one of the best-conditioned players on that team." I wish him well because he is a good football player and a good guy.

Back in New Orleans, things were moving along very well at the Superdome. Repairs were on schedule, if not ahead of schedule. One of the most obvious signs of the incredible progress going on was the massive white roof of the Superdome. As July came to an end, and attention began to focus more closely on the team, workers at the dome put the finishing touches on it, and the skyline of the city was whole once again.

Mitch Landrieu, *lieutenant governor, Louisiana*

The average guy on the street didn't really have any idea what was going on inside the Superdome. Of course, we—meaning government officials and the people at the dome, Tim Coulon, Doug Thornton, and their staffs—knew how well it was going. But for the people to see that roof just as white as could be, that gave them a little boost. It raised their confidence level.

Mickey Loomis

There was still lingering doubt in the minds of some people that they really couldn't get the Superdome back open in time. We had calls at the ticket office asking if we were sure that it would be ready in time for that Monday night game. But once the roof was finished, and people could see that, well, they sort of knew it was real.

Pam Randazza, *owner, Black & Gold Sports Shop*

It was another little bump, a little push, you know? It seemed every few weeks something positive would come along and get the people more excited. We all kept seeing the roof coming together, and then when it was finished, you could just kind of imagine that the inside must be like that, too. That's when the people really knew they were coming back. That roof being nice again was something they could see that was tangible.

Bobby Hebert

Our studios were right next door to the Superdome, so we saw it getting fixed more and more every day. It was like it was all coming back to life. People needed to see that.

Doug Thornton, *general manager, Superdome*

You had to know how bad it had been in here to see how far we had come. It was just inspiring how much we were getting done. We had hundreds of guys here working long hours. Suppliers were getting us the things we needed where we thought we might not be able to get them at all.

You can see the roof of the Superdome from just about everywhere in town, and half the people in town have to drive past it every day. So, as we got closer to getting the roof finished, people could see that we were going to be okay, that we were getting it done.

We were working at full throttle in late July when Paul Tagliabue gave us the official look-over. Governor Blanco was here, and of course Tom Benson.

Paul Tagliabue, *NFL commissioner*

I wanted to thank all of the men and women in hard hats who were getting the work done. There were really some terrific new features being done in the renovation that had been done from the standpoint of the fans who would be enjoying Saints games that season. The whole building has terrific new features that have been put in under very difficult circumstances.

Tom Benson, *owner, New Orleans Saints*

We were very pleased about how the renovation was coming along. We knew it was going to be inspiring for the people of Louisiana and the Gulf Coast to show the people of the country what we have done and what we will continue to do.

Paul Tagliabue

Was I surprised by what I saw? Yes, I was. On my prior visits here, there had been some concern about the availability of materials and a skilled labor force and there had been disputes about funding. It seemed like all of those things had been worked out in a very commonsense and positive way.

Mickey Loomis

Commissioner Tagliabue was very impressed by what he saw there that day. I think that if he had any doubts about whether or not the Superdome could be ready in time, they had been put to rest. We were proud of what we were doing in camp, too.

Sammy Marten, *fan*

When I was a lot younger, the team held training camp right in Hammond, so I had watched a training camp before. Jackson is not that far from where I live in Memphis, so a few times I jumped in my little truck and drove down to watch them. They had been so bad in 2005 that you just didn't know what to expect. But I liked Drew Brees right away, and the whole atmosphere there just felt good. They seemed confident.

And fans were coming from everywhere. People forget that the

Saints aren't only about New Orleans. They have fans all over Memphis and Mississippi. There are a few people in Memphis I guess who like the Titans, but mostly the people I know like the Saints. The parking lot at training camp had license plates from Louisiana and Mississippi. There were Tennessee plates. I even saw Alabama and Texas.

Kenny Wilkerson

One of the big questions was how Deuce was going to react to Reggie Bush being here. You know, Ricky Williams had really not been that nice to Deuce. Ricky was condescending to Deuce in a lot of ways. They were both first-round draft choices, but Ricky was the star at that time.

Well, that got answered right away, too. Deuce just went out of his way to put Reggie at ease. He could have been a jerk, but if you know Deuce, you knew that wouldn't be the case.

Reggie Bush

I always knew it would be something of an adjustment coming into the NFL, and so it took a little while to get used to training camp and pro football, but my teammates made me feel welcome. Especially Deuce. For Deuce to embrace me like he did was just so welcoming, because he could have easily felt threatened by me—you know, a young rookie coming in with all the money and hype behind him. Nobody would have blamed him if he had felt threatened, but he didn't. He welcomed me with open arms, and that, to me, said a lot about him and the type of guy he is.

Sean Payton

That was really big, Deuce being like he was with Reggie. There could have been tension, but it just shows you what he's made of. He's a real gentleman and a great player. He defines what you want on your team. He really understood what being on a team means. I really respect Deuce.

I think it was also good for Reggie that we were in Jackson and not in New Orleans. I wanted training camp somewhere that would allow the team to focus. We had to come together as a team and prepare, and we were able to do that there at Millsaps College. Reggie is very disciplined, but being in a smaller town on a small campus really let him focus on what he had to do without as much media coverage as there might have been in New Orleans.

Drew Brees, *quarterback, New Orleans Saints*

It was great having training camp in Jackson. Guys had been accustomed to working out at the home facility and being close to everything. I think Coach Payton did a great job of getting guys away from town and making it a place where we could focus, where we could come together as a team, where we can eliminate distractions, and where we can really cultivate this new culture with our team. A new attitude, a winning attitude.

Kenny Wilkerson

Just before the preseason games you could see that they were doing pretty well compared to other training camps I had covered, and I've been covering training camps since the late eighties. I'm not saying we had any idea that this team was going to become what it became, but there was a little something there.

Scott Fujita, *linebacker, New Orleans Saints*

You never really know what to expect until guys start getting some game time together, and that is what you do in preseason. So it worked well for us. We were all in camp and we had been working together and coming together as a team, and then here we were with the Titans game.

Mickey Loomis

The fans don't always like or understand why we have the preseason games, but we need them. We have to see what these guys can do; we have to try different things out. Decisions have to be made, and you can't make those just by watching guys in practice playing against each other. We had so many things to look at in that first preseason game against Tennessee.

Kenny Wilkerson

It goes without saying that everybody was watching Drew Brees and Reggie Bush. Drew hadn't been in a game since he hurt his shoulder, and there was all the hype about Reggie. So, even though it was preseason, a lot of people were watching.

Sean Payton

One of the most important things in that game was to get Drew back on the field. I liked what I saw. There were plenty of positive things, and some things to work on. Overall, it was good for Drew to be back in live action and get this step out of the way so he could move on.

Drew Brees

We came out with scores on two out of three drives. The first two drives weren't very good, but we were able to get down the field and get a field goal. The third drive, I thought we had a chance to get down there and get a touchdown, but we came up a little short.

Kenny Wilkerson

Drew hooked up with Joe Horn a couple of times and they were, you know, okay. Reggie caught a pass on the first series, which was a little surprising because we were expecting him to run first. Looking back, I guess it should have told us something about how they would use him in the regular season.

Then, the second time the Saints had possession, Reggie got the ball and was heading left when all of a sudden he cuts and runs right and goes down the sideline for 44 yards. Everybody had been waiting to see what he could do, and they didn't have to wait long. There it was. By the time he came out he had run for about 60 yards and caught a pair of passes for another 10. Right there it sort of set the tone for what he would do all season.

Sean Payton

Reggie had some big plays in the running game. He's the type of guy that can bring big plays, and we saw some of that potential that night.

Reggie Bush

It was a pretty productive day. I got my feet wet, and we won the game, which is the most important thing.

Sean Payton

Against Dallas up in Shreveport, I was a little disappointed that there wasn't much good that happened. I don't think our first team played that well on either side of the ball. The second half wasn't much better.

Drew Brees

We had three three-and-outs in that game, which was unacceptable. That was not the type of offense we wanted to be. The emphasis has to be on starting fast, and that has to be an attitude. Once we get that initial first down, then we know that we can roll down the field.

Kenny Wilkerson

The last real question left was about Deuce, and he finally played against Dallas that night. He looked good. He had looked good in camp, and he looked okay there. He only ran the ball twice, but at least you saw he could run.

Deuce McAllister, *running back, New Orleans Saints*

It felt good to be out there against another defense. I felt fine, and the knee was good.

Kenny Wilkerson

Other than that, they looked awful. They were getting blown away at the line of scrimmage and everything. They ended up losing 30–7. We all just thought, wow, this could really suck.

Back at camp, we were all just thinking, well, here we go again. But then they started making moves. They did a deal with Dallas to get Scott Shanle at linebacker. Two linebackers from Dallas and both named Scott: Scott Fujita and now Scott Shanle.

Scott Shanle, *linebacker, New Orleans Saints*

I was really excited when I found out I was going to New Orleans. I got a call from Coach Parcells, and he said he had gotten me into a good situation. Man, he was right. It's a big factor when you come to a team to feel comfortable. Knowing Coach Payton and Coach Gibbs, I felt real comfortable with them.

Sean Payton

Here was another quality player that could step right in and play. Gary Gibbs and I had both worked with Scott, and so we had a real good idea what we were getting with him.

Scott Shanle

Anytime you have a team who makes a trade for you, they are expecting you to come in and contribute to the team. That was what I was looking to do.

Kenny Wilkerson

So then Peyton Manning and the Colts come to Jackson, and it looks just as bad as the Dallas game. The Saints turned the ball over five times. It was horrendous.

Sean Payton

The thing I told the team was, when you play a game like that, when you turn the ball over five times, you are not going to win in this league. You just can't win like that. So the first thing we had to address were the turnovers. I didn't want anybody dismissing that because it was preseason, because it's about more than that. We needed to start doing something. I was really disappointed that night.

Drew Brees

This just wasn't what I knew we were capable of. I knew we could be better than that. We were better than that. We had to get it going.

Sean Payton

We had one preseason game left, and in two weeks we were playing in the regular season. We were not a ready product, and you could see that watching us.

Kenny Wilkerson

The only real thing worth talking about in that game was Deuce showing that he was back at full strength. He got 67 yards, and 27 of that came when he broke one down the sidelines. Then on the next play he went 15 yards for a touchdown. He's from Mississippi, so getting himself going again there in Jackson meant a lot.

Deuce McAllister

I felt like I could run the ball. It was all about getting out there and getting into a rhythm and making plays. From that point, as far as getting into the end zone, I think all of the guys were excited for me.

Kenny Wilkerson

Keep in mind that they still got their butts handed to them. They lost that one 27–14. And then they started making moves again.

By this time, Marques Colston was starting to look really good. And with Joe Horn and Devery Henderson, they were kind of stacked at wide receiver. Donte Stallworth was pretty vocal about not really being happy here, and so out he goes to Philadelphia and in comes Mark Simoneau at linebacker. Now they have four guys who can really play linebacker, but only Fujita had come into training camp with the team.

Sean Payton

We traded Donte for Mark. The feeling was that we had some depth at the wide receiver position with some of the young guys playing so well. Marques was really turning out to be special, as were all of our guys. I think it was also good to give Donte a fresh start in Philadelphia and for us to acquire a quality player like Mark.

Kenny Wilkerson

In what ended up being a revolving-door-type deal all season, they had to let Fred McAfee go. He was a real star on special teams. Everybody loves Freddie. It was tough, but he kept coming back all season. Gone, then back, and then gone, then back.

Sean Payton

It was the hardest cut I had to make. Fred's a special person and the kind of guy you look for, as far as character goes. He is always smiling, even when we had to let him go, which we did more than once that season. Of course, he smiled a lot more when we brought him back.

Mickey Loomis

We had a very special opportunity just after the team closed camp and came back to New Orleans. The president was in town to mark the one-year anniversary of Katrina, and we were asked to go to the airport and meet him.

Reggie Bush

We were like old friends. I had met him after we won the national championship at USC in 2004. Back then, my nickname was "the president," and so we kidded each other about that. And, you know, we're both named Bush. It was fun.

Sean Payton

It meant a lot to our guys, and it really brought home to the new guys how big what had happened here had been. Some of these guys were just coming to New Orleans for the first time. They had joined us in training camp. So, meeting the president was real important. I gave George Bush a white jersey with the number 43 and BUSH on it.

Joe Horn, *wide receiver, New Orleans Saints*

I got to introduce President Bush to the team. I don't always agree
with the man, but he is our president, my president. If you are an
American, then the president is the president, and he deserves respect. It was a big moment for me being able to do that.

Kenny Wilkerson

So they go to Kansas City for the final preseason game. It is just not
real exciting, and Sean Payton is kind of standing around like a
statue. But then all of a sudden it was like somebody threw on a
switch. He started really taking control. It was something we really
hadn't seen before in the preseason games.

Maybe he had made his cuts and this was really his team now
and it was like, okay, now we're going to show you what we can
really do.

And then we start seeing Drew Brees doing the same thing. All
of a sudden he's all into it on the sidelines. Not fighting or anything,
not arguing, but just taking control of things.

Drew Brees

I remember a moment. In fact, it was right after we played the Colts
in the preseason. A couple of times we showed greatness, but then
we were falling short. We had gotten beaten pretty badly. But I realized that we were going to be okay. I went up to guys on the sidelines
and was like, "Don't worry. We're going to be okay." By the Kansas
City game, I felt really confident, very confident, about where we
were going as a team.

Steve Gleason

We had a meeting with just the players. Drew got up and went over the goals for us as a team. It was really good. It was like he was saying, "I'm your man. I am going to be the leader here. Let's get it together now."

And everybody was on board with that. They were like, "Drew, all right, you're our man. If you're going to lead us, we're going with you."

And from that moment, just before the season started, we were suddenly this "team." Drew was a leader, and he was going to lead us. I hadn't seen anything like that in my six years in New Orleans. Man, it was a great feeling. It was something that had been lacking in this franchise, and now it was going to be different.

Bobby Hebert

That is really why I am such a big supporter of Drew Brees. He let everybody know that he was the leader. He is the quarterback. He has to be. Sometimes on teams there isn't a guy like that. It makes a big difference.

It really doesn't matter that they lost to the Chiefs in that last game in the preseason. Coach Payton was leading them, and Drew Brees was leading them. That's how you want it, and to be getting there right then, well, the timing was perfect. They were on a wave that was cresting just at the right time.

Joe Horn

I respect Drew Brees. He didn't play any favorites. He wasn't about throwing to this one guy or that one guy. I'm a competitor, you know? I want every pass to come to me. But I know that sometimes somebody else might be in a better position to make something happen, so that's who should get the ball. And Drew Brees, he always threw to the man who had the possibilities to make the plays. On that team, there were no stars and All Stars, all at the same time.

THE SAINTS ARE COMING

AFTER A STRONG but uneventful training camp and a lackluster preseason, the Saints returned home to New Orleans. There had been the usual media opportunities and a visit with President George W. Bush. The team and the players had answered the key questions: Yes, Drew Brees's shoulder was okay, and he had established himself as a leader. Yes, Deuce was back to his old form. And yes, Reggie Bush was showing signs of the greatness everyone had hoped for. The team had done its part.

The brilliant white roof of the Superdome put an end to any doubts that the centerpiece of the city and the home of the Saints would be ready. There was more excitement about it than when it had first opened three decades before. The people wanted to get inside and see how it looked. In many ways, the dome was a kind of home for the people here. It had become a symbol of rebirth and had inspired many to fix their own homes.

Now it was time for the fans to do their part. They had to support the team.

They had to rise above all that had happened to them and around them and rally around the Saints. And they did it in incredible ways.

Mickey Loomis, *general manager, New Orleans Saints*

Season-ticket sales had been moving along pretty well, especially after hiring Sean Payton. After that, we had a few spikes. Obviously, signing Drew caused a spike, and then signing Reggie was another big spike. So, sales had been strong, but I think seeing the dome coming along really solidified it all in the fans' minds.

Pam Randazza, *owner, Black & Gold Sports Shop*

So many people in my store were talking about actually going to the games. They had tickets. I know we've had people in here before who had tickets, but now it seemed like everybody had them.

Jack Catalinotto, *fan*

In the aftermath of Hurricane Katrina, I lost my insurance agency when my company decided to stop writing new policies in southern Louisiana. I took what work I could find and got a temporary storm-related job as a debris monitor in St. Tammany Parish. I was just happy to assist in the cleanup while earning a living for my family.

I was listening to the car radio when the team introduced Sean Payton as head coach. I remember being impressed with his businesslike approach and his sincerity in setting a goal of bringing a winning attitude to the team and to the city. The acquisition of Drew Brees restored my faith in the management of the team, and of course, the shock of the draft in our getting Reggie Bush all pointed me in one direction: the purchase of season tickets. So, with a little extra money that accidentally fell our way, I bought four season tickets. After a long divorce from the team where I thought it would wallow in mediocrity forever, we were back together. And I thought, wow, what a wonderful birthday it will be for me on September 25th when the Saints come marching back into the dome! And to face the Dirty Birds at that!

Steve Gleason, *safety, New Orleans Saints*

My girlfriend's family is all from New Orleans. Most of them live in Lakeview, which was really ground zero for the levees breaking. They all had fifteen or sixteen feet of water in their houses and lost everything, but they all still bought season tickets.

Mitch Landrieu, *lieutenant governor, Louisiana*

The people just needed something. They needed something to celebrate and to feel good about.

Doug Thornton, *general manager, Superdome*

I was surprised and not surprised. Here you are with half of the population you had before the storm and people still gutting out their homes and just going through so much, and they feel so strongly about this team and what it represented that they start buying season tickets in record numbers.

Mickey Loomis

Our ticket people kept telling us that there really were not many tickets left for any of the games, but when they finally told us that they were all gone, that we were 100% sold out for the entire season,

I was really taken aback. I was shocked. Mr. Benson was really moved and wanted to personally speak to the fans and the community.

Tom Benson, *owner, New Orleans Saints*

There had been so many negative stories after Hurricane Katrina that I felt compelled to come out and talk about a positive story: our team and our fans and their support as we started the 2006 campaign. This was the first time in our team's forty-year history that this had happened. And all of the credit goes to the fans. That is a positive story.

We had spoken so many times about the return of football to the Superdome and what this would symbolize, but we didn't need to look any further than the resolve of our fans in this community and the way they rallied around this team. There were many stories the week we returned to the Superdome, but I think the real story was our fans, the people who lived through this terrible tragedy, their own return, and their return to the Superdome as well, in record numbers.

This was the start of something good in our city. We had been working hard on the field and off the field out in the community. As I spoke, Reggie Bush and a host of other players were at it again downtown donating four tons of food to over 800 needy families. These are special things that mean so much to me as the owner of this team.

Scott Fujita, *linebacker, New Orleans Saints*

I had moved into a place in the warehouse district right downtown, so I had felt the pulse of the city and I knew it was getting upbeat, but I was really dumbstruck when I heard that we were sold out for the season. I had by no means expected that. It just made the city and the fans that much more special.

Drew Brees, *quarterback, New Orleans Saints*

It just inspired me more. If these people can overcome what they have, then I have to get my job done. I have to do it for myself and for my teammates and really turn it up for these people. They had done more than their share, so we had to do ours.

Sammy Marten, *fan*

I was screwed! I usually call around my old buddies or my brothers or somebody to get tickets when I want to go see the Saints. Or I can call and order on the phone if I have to. I mean, I was happy that they sold out and all, but how was I supposed to get in? They could have warned me, you know? "Hey, Sammy, buddy, you better get your ass down here and buy some tickets because they're going fast."

Kenny Wilkerson, *sideline reporter, WWL Radio*

So, now it's really showtime. I mean, the season is here and it's time to put up or shut up, you know? First up is Cleveland.

Doug Thornton

I think if we had needed to, we could have hosted that first game against Cleveland, but I was glad to have that little bit of time to really get things ready.

Sean Payton, *head coach, New Orleans Saints*

Our first training camp had just finished, and our first week of the regular season was coming up. You look at the schedule and make sure you're not missing anything. You get into a routine. It was the first game of the season and my main concern was eliminating the things that prevent us from winning games, turnovers, and producing some turnovers on defense. That had been the one thing that had concerned me during the preseason.

In the first game of the 2006 season, the Saints defeated the Cleveland Browns 19–14. They did it largely on the strength of sure-footed, seventeen-year veteran John Carney. On top of a 12-yard touchdown pass from Drew Brees to the emerging Marques Colston, Carney's 4 field goals made the difference. The team also converted several key third-down situations.

Consistent contributions from veterans Deuce McAllister, Joe Horn, and Ernie Conwell blended with those of the team's new players. Rookie standouts included Reggie Bush and his 141 all-purpose yards, and Jahri Evans, the fourth-rounder who stepped into the right-guard spot and more than held his own. Second-round pick Roman Harper also earned high marks with 5 tackles and a fourth-quarter sack.

Proving themselves the most dangerous tandem in the NFL, Deuce and Reggie combined for 151 yards on the ground. And Drew Brees, in full control of his team, spread the ball around to multiple receivers for 4 receptions, including the touchdown.

The defensive line, with Hollis Thomas in the middle, kept pressure up front and allowed linebackers Mark Simoneau, Scott Shanle, and Scott Fujita to catch the ball carriers who came their way. It was a solid game from a group of players who had just come together in the closing weeks of training camp. With that win, Coach Sean Payton became only the second head coach in the team's history to win his season opener, the first since Dick Nolan in 1978.

Sean Payton

I was excited for the players and for the fans of New Orleans. I was excited for all of the people that I had come across who really looked forward to watching this team. I knew it had to feel good for them to see us win. And it was important for me as the coach and for these players that we get that first win under our belts.

Drew Brees

It was huge to get that win. Anytime you have to go on the road to play, it's definitely a hostile environment and very hard to come out with a victory. So for us to be able to do that with our first game on the road just reinforced that attitude and culture of winning.

Abbe Garfinkel, *fan*

I have to be honest. I had given up on the Saints two years before. I'd just written them off. I was like, that's it. I'm not buying into it ever again. Every year they would convince me that this was a new team and that they were really going to do it, and they would break your heart. Every year.

It had gotten to the point that when they hired Sean Payton I had started cutting out his pictures from the newspapers and sticking them on the refrigerator, because I knew that he was going down in flames just like everybody else. I just didn't want to like him. He has those gleamy little eyes and those pert lips and they just always seem to get tighter and tighter. He seemed like a priss.

But we listen to Bobby Hebert and Kenny Wilkerson every day—"the boys"—and they kept saying that this team and this coach were different. I was living in my FEMA trailer twenty feet from my house, which had been devastated by the hurricane. I had all of these insurance hassles and contractors screwing with me, and there was all of this bad news everywhere. So, maybe because they were the bright spot, the good news, I gave Payton a shot. I was like, "Okay, it's your funeral, Sean. But I'll watch."

I did, and they won. It was the first good time I'd had in that damn trailer.

Reggie Bush, *running back, New Orleans Saints*

I was real excited and honored to be chosen Diet Pepsi NFL Rookie of the Week after that game in Cleveland. It was really a reflection of our team though, especially the hard work of our offensive line and my offensive teammates. I think credit also had to go to our defense for an outstanding performance that allowed us to keep running all day.

Sean Payton

As big as getting that first win was for everybody, we had to get ready for Green Bay. Lambeau Field is a real tough place to play.

Reggie Bush

Coach Payton had reminded us all week to be thinking about that week's game in Green Bay and not any further. Although we were excited about how we played in Cleveland, looking back or looking ahead a couple of weeks can get you in trouble as an individual and as a team. The entire focus was on Green Bay.

For the second game of the season, the Saints traveled to Green Bay, Wisconsin, to face Brett Favre and the Packers. Historic and imposing Lambeau Field is a place where legends are made. It was only fitting that the legend of the 2006 New Orleans Saints would begin here.

In boxing, a true champion is measured not by how many wins and knockouts he compiles. Champions respond to adversity. They rise up from the canvas just as they're about to be counted out, beating the odds to claim victory. The Saints, as a team, showed a strong chin and a tremendous heart against the Packers.

On the Saints' first possession, Drew Brees was sacked, and he fumbled. Five plays later, Brett Favre completed a 22-yard touchdown pass to receiver Greg Jennings. On the Saints' next series, the Packers stripped Drew Brees of the pigskin while he was being sacked, again. Just three plays later, kicker Dave Rayner extended the Packers' lead to 10–0 with a 24-yard field goal.

Brees's third drive seemed to be the charm. He led the Saints from their own 19-yard line down to the Packers' 24 in just 9 plays. But they failed again. A batted-down pass was intercepted by cornerback Al Harris. Favre then drove the Packers' offense 75 yards in 8 plays to set up another Rayner field goal.

Suddenly, it seemed that this Saints team would be no different from those of the past. That despite all of the hoopla and goodwill of the preceding months, they didn't have what it took to win in the NFL. Everybody had that feeling—everybody except the players on the field.

As a team, and to a man, they did not panic. Sean Payton stayed true to his offensive plan of a mixed assault on the ground and in the air. With their next possession, Brees connected to Bush on a key third down, followed shortly by a lightning-strike 30-yard pass to tight end Mark Campbell. That brought the boys in black and gold down to the 3-yard line. Just 2 plays later, with a block from Jamar Nesbit, Deuce forced his way into the end zone for his first touchdown since September 25 of the 2005 season.

After holding Favre and company in check and forcing a punt, the Saints began the go-ahead drive, capped off by a 26-yard touchdown reception by Devery Henderson. Two subsequent drives were capped by Carney field goals, and one of them featured a 47-yard reception by Joe Horn, which put the cagey veteran over 7,000 yards in his career. The Saints were now in control of the game and their destiny, at 20–13.

Brett Favre would add to his well-deserved legend with a rallying drive that tied the score at 20–20. Not to be outdone by the Packers great, Drew Brees tossed a picture-perfect 35-yard pass to the well-covered Marques Colston for a touchdown. The Saints' Will Smith ended any hopes of a Packers comeback when he recovered an Ahman Green fumble at the Green Bay 23. One play later, Deuce McAllister tore the turf for a 20-yard touchdown. The Packers scored a late touchdown, but their fate had been sealed.

The game would end with the scoreboard reading Saints 34, Packers 27. But as would be the case so many times in this storybook season, the real story was not on any scoreboard. It was in the hearts of the team and its fans.

Steve Gleason

Nothing is impossible, nothing. It is only impossible in your mind, and only if you let it be. It might have been impossible to previous Saints teams, but not to this one. We were down and maybe counted out, but winning that game was not impossible. Not one guy believed it was impossible, and so it was possible. And from possible, it became a reality. After we won under those circumstances, I felt, the whole team felt, that everything was possible now.

Kenny Wilkerson

Well, you just had to be blown away. I can't even think of how many times the old Saints would have just been over and done with right there in the first quarter. Payton and Brees and the whole team just kept coming and coming.

Sean Payton

That was really going against the numbers, turning the ball over three times in the first quarter on the road. That was one of the things we really needed to correct, but give our players credit, they hung in there.

Drew Brees

Maybe that was a better win than if we had just won straight up with no problems. Don't get me wrong, you want to win. You always want to win, but battling from behind like we did, it showed us something about ourselves that we needed to see as a team. It was very emotional. It was a great feeling to have come together and won like that.

Bobby Hebert, *former quarterback, New Orleans Saints*

Maybe the fans don't know, but it is hard to come back. A lot of coaches, you know, they get behind and they start getting desperate with the play calling. When you do that, it is like telling your players, "We can't win like we thought we could." It ripples, and then they start panicking, too. Coach Payton just kept doing what he had planned. Maybe he changed a play here or there, but they were just doing what they do best.

Joe Horn, *wide receiver, New Orleans Saints*

They told me or made an announcement that I had gone 7,000 yards, but man, you can't be thinking about that in the middle of a game. Seven thousand? Great, let me get some more. That's how you have to think. I was just glad to be out there and being a part of us getting that win. If we had lost that one, a lot of things might have been different. The story of the season might have been different.

Sammy Marten

In the first quarter, I had thought, look at these sorry pieces of crap. They looked just as bad as ever. They had beaten *Cleveland*. So what? They were stinking up Green Bay like the nasty cheese they make there. Cheeseheads. Give me a break, will you? But then my boy Drew just stays cool and—bam, bam, bam—they come right back and win it.

Abbe Garfinkel

Our FEMA trailer is not much bigger than a refrigerator. While they were fumbling the game away in the first quarter, I was shouting, "Here they go again! Here they go again!" I wanted to get up and go into another room—but we don't have any other rooms.

Every time they showed Sean Payton, those little lips were just getting tighter and tighter and tighter, like they were going to break or snap. But, you gotta hand it to him. He never lost it. How many Saints coaches can you say that about?

And Drew Brees? Wow! I mean, is he great or what? He could have just quit and nobody would have blamed him, not in this city at least.

Like I said, my old house is just twenty feet from the trailer. I had so much adrenaline built up after the game that I had to do something, so I went in the house and started hauling stuff out. We had been waiting for weeks for the guys to come get this stuff out so we could get some work done, to start rebuilding in there. Well, I guess thanks to the Saints I at least got the trash out of my house.

Greg Bensel, *vice president, public relations, New Orleans Saints*

When we got back to New Orleans that night, there were hundreds if not thousands of fans lined up outside of the airport. The players and the coaches signed autographs and waved. They just couldn't thank the fans enough. They had come out that night and displayed their passion and we all began looking forward to our big game at the Superdome.

Sean Payton

This was my first homecoming, if you will, as the Saints coach. I had been told that there might be some fans there, but I really wasn't prepared for it. It was nice and a good feeling.

Scott Fujita

Yeah, it really just brought it home. It was like, okay, here they are. These are our fans. This is who it's about.

Joe Horn

I saw all kinds of people that night, some with little kids, all smiling and cheering. Don't take this the wrong way, but people in crowds start to look a lot alike. So, to me, it was like I was seeing the same people I had seen back in Texas at the Astrodome and in Wal-Mart and places like that. They were letting us know that they needed us and they were with us. I said to myself, "Okay, now let us go get us some Falcons."

10

OUR HOME. OUR TEAM. BE A SAINT.

AS THE SAINTS flew back from Green Bay with a spotless record of 2–0, what had seemed impossible just months before was now a reality: The team was coming home. Once black and blue, New Orleans was now black and shiny gold. Once tattered and torn, the roof of the Superdome now gleamed its whitest white. And in the place where thousands of miserable, lost souls had once desperately sought refuge, now stood tens of thousands anxiously seeking victory and hope. Huge banners draped the dome, reading: "Our home. Our team. Be a Saint." It was as if the Superdome, for this one very special moment, was the center of the universe.

New Orleans, being New Orleans, knows how to celebrate like no place on earth, and this would be a celebration to beat them all. The Superdome was back. The Saints were back. New Orleans was back, and the world was watching.

Doug Thornton, *general manager, Superdome*

I had been saying that we would be "football ready" for opening night, and we were. The suites were not finished. The floors in the club level were not finished. The paint may have still been wet in some places, but we were ready for football.

Mitch Landrieu, *lieutenant governor, Louisiana*

Doug Thornton was the man in charge, and he certainly got it done. But he also had a lot of support. It was a real team effort. Doug was like the coach. It really was amazing to see the Superdome looking as good as it did. I think, it many ways, it was actually better than before.

Dave Dixon, *"Father of the Superdome"*

I had been inside the Superdome a day or so before, and it really looked good. It was just as pretty as the day it had opened. I couldn't wait to see it filled with fans again.

Quint Davis, *founder and producer, New Orleans Jazz & Heritage Festival*

I knew, we all knew, that it was going to be a very special, emotional day in the city, and it had to have a New Orleans feel and flavor to it. This really wasn't about the NFL coming here; it was about all of us coming back. Really, I think I was just as eager and excited as anybody. I am a huge Saints fan, so I couldn't wait.

Mickey Loomis, *general manager, New Orleans Saints*

I had been following the progress at the Superdome and was getting really excited. I felt we had the makings of a pretty good ball club, and so as we got closer to that game I knew I felt good. And seeing the city and the fans getting that excited, well, it was just something special.

Kenny Wilkerson, *sideline reporter, WWL Radio*

I gotta be honest. I had real doubts that anybody would even go back into the place after what had gone on during Katrina. There were so many stories, mostly BS, but a lot of them true. A lot of people thought that maybe they just wouldn't reopen it. If you had seen what it was really like in there before, you couldn't imagine that it could ever be nice again.

And there was so much speculation that the team was gone, too. Hosting the show with Bobby Hebert every day, you know, I get told more information than most fans or people in the city, and I really thought for a while that the Saints were never coming back. I had hoped they would and all, but now it really was happening.

Quint Davis

I had worked with the Saints on concerts and that sort of thing before, and I really wanted to be part of this event. I don't know who called who first, but I can tell you I was already, in my head, thinking about what I could do to make this fun for the fans. New Orleans loves music and festivals. So naturally we were going to have one for this. I mean, *everybody* wanted to be part of it.

From the beginning there was going to be music, and we thought it would be Allen Toussaint and Elvis Costello; they had done some really great work together on their CD, and the proceeds of that had benefited a lot of people. So that's the level I was working on. The league and the network people thought it should be bigger. I was thinking, this *is* big, but they wanted something that would draw better on TV.

Then, The Edge from U2 got involved, and he wanted to perform. Well, that was tremendous. I could see that this was going to get bigger and bigger. We were getting calls from everywhere. It looked like The Edge and about ten of the best guitarists in the world would all play together in this huge jam session. That's what we started planning on.

I remember I was in my car, and I got a call on my cell. I heard a voice say, "We got them. It's all set."

"Got who?"

"U2 and Green Day."

"What? We have who?"

I mean, I was just amazed, you know?

I still wanted something New Orleans in there, so I said that we should have Allen Toussaint and Irma Thomas sing the national anthem. The league and the network wanted somebody else. They said that Allen and Irma were "too New Orleans." Too New Orleans? For Christ's sake, come on, this *is* New Orleans. Isn't this *for* New Orleans?

In the end they agreed, and it was terrific. I think it really helped set the tone for the whole evening. It let everybody around the world know that: This is New Orleans. This is who we are. And I think it gave our people a taste of what they had been missing. A lot of our fans had lost everything and were scattered all over the place. They couldn't be here for the game, so to see Irma made them feel good. She is as New Orleans as it gets. Everybody loves Irma. She's the Soul Queen of New Orleans.

Kenny Wilkerson

Look, I was a fan for a long time before I ever thought about being a reporter. I'm from New Orleans. I grew up watching the Saints. So I was not just getting excited as a reporter who covers the team, I was frickin' excited, you know what I mean? And by being this close to it, talking to fans every day as it got closer, I knew it was really going to be big.

Everywhere you looked, people wearing Saints stuff. I have never seen so many fleurs-de-lis. They were everywhere. In the days leading up to that game, I think the people who weren't wearing Saints gear stuck out more than the people who were. I'm talking lawyers and doctors and big businesspeople all walking around in it.

I went to buy some things for myself, and the stores were all running out of stuff. They even put out old Aaron Brooks jerseys, and people were buying those. They were buying anything that had the Saints on it.

Pam Randazza, *owner, Black & Gold Sports Shop*

The fever, if you want to call it that, had really started when they hired Sean Payton, and it just got bigger and bigger. Even in the preseason, when they didn't really play all that well, we were selling a lot of stuff. After we won those first two games, it really started getting crazy around here.

The week of the Falcons game, with the dome reopening, I have never seen anything like that, ever. I showed up in the morning and there were already people lined up outside, a couple hundred. My store isn't that big, and I normally don't have that many employees. I had to let people in so many at a time, let them get what they wanted, and then let some more in. The line outside just kept getting longer. The more people I let in, the more people showed up.

And the fans, they weren't just buying one thing. They were buying everything, everything we had. I know that a lot of these people had lost everything. They were living in those FEMA trailers, fighting with their insurance companies. Most of them, bless their hearts, hadn't had anything to be excited about in a long time. To see them all happy, well, it made me feel really good about my part in all of this. You could see it on their faces—they needed it. It is my business, and it's how I make my living and all, but that week it almost felt like I was doing a public service.

People kept telling me that I could raise the prices, that I could charge more and that the fans would still buy everything, but I couldn't do that to these people. No way. Not a chance. I wish I could have given it to them for free. Of course I couldn't do that, but I wasn't going to take advantage, either. In fact, I hired more people to work here and a lot of them had lost everything, too. So the excitement over the Saints benefited people in a lot of different ways.

Bobby Hebert, *former quarterback, New Orleans Saints*

I was just so happy for the fans. And when I say the fans, I really mean everybody in New Orleans, because, at least at that moment, everybody here was a fan. Some people had said, "Oh, who cares about the Saints? Why waste all that money to fix the Superdome? Let them go to San Antonio or wherever." Well, now everybody was a Saints fan, because they meant so much to the city and all. You'd have to be a Scrooge to not feel good about all of this.

Kenny Wilkerson

We usually get a lot of calls to the show, but once that game got close we had people calling in long before the show even started, just so they could try to get on. It was like a nonstop pep rally.

Sammy Marten, *fan*

My brother had tickets to the Falcons game. I kept hounding him, hoping that somebody from his family wasn't going to go, but they all wanted to go. We have a big family; if he'd had 100 tickets, we would have used them all. So I was just gonna watch the game in Memphis with some buddies.

Then, that morning, I started watching the television and listening to WWL. You can hear it all over the South because it has like 50,000 watts, whatever that means. So I was listening, and I got the fever real bad. It's early in the morning, and they're talking about the game already. I just couldn't take it anymore. I grabbed my Saints gear and jumped in my truck and headed south. I was eating drive-thru and hauling ass. I got to New Orleans by early afternoon and just took the first place I could find to park my car.

Sean Payton, *head coach, New Orleans Saints*

In the weeks leading up to those first two games, I kept telling the team how big that Falcons game was going to be. A lot of the guys had never played in a home game there, so maybe they didn't know just how big it was going to be. To be frank, I had never coached a home game there, so I really didn't know how big it was going to be, either.

I had told the team it would really be incredible if they could go into that home opener a 2–0 record. And so by winning those two games, well, I just knew that this was going to be really something special.

Mickey Loomis

I've been in football for a long time, and I have never felt anything like it. It's all anybody was talking about. I always knew that the Saints and the people here had a very special relationship, but this really brought it home.

People don't always realize that we have a lot of people who work for us in sales, the front office, marketing, and so forth. Even if we had not seen what it meant to the fans, we could all see how much it meant to our own people. Many of them had their lives turned inside and out, and so this was really something special and unique for them.

Joe Horn, *wide receiver, New Orleans Saints*

I live in New Orleans year-round, so I knew. This was more than just a football game to these people. This was it for them. I had been pretty vocal before about how important it was that we get back to New Orleans. Here we were, just like we said we would be, and, man, did they respond. This was all about the people. We were just a symbol, something you could see. For us to come back, well, for them it was like they had come back, too.

Mickey Loomis

I don't know if I could really describe what it was like in New Orleans that week. The season was already 100% sold out, and that was a first in franchise history. We were getting calls from everywhere with people looking for tickets. There just weren't any.

Sammy Marten

I didn't have a ticket or anything, just my black and gold. I had a Deuce jersey on and black pants. I was going to try and meet my brothers later, but the party had already started down by the dome, and I just joined in. It was like everybody was old friends. People were just handing me beer and food and everything. So I was drinking the free beer and dancing and having a good old time.

No matter where you went, it seemed like all they were playing was Saints songs. It was like one guy had a CD and made fifty copies and that's all anybody was playing. Even the radio stations.

There wasn't much car traffic down there because people were dancing in the streets and all. I made my way over to the Superdome. I'm not sure if you were supposed to have a ticket to get up by the concert, but I got there without one. The clock was ticking down and everybody was just laughing and having a good time. You know us, we love to party.

Doug Thornton

We've had many, many really big events here at the dome. We've hosted a lot of Super Bowls, national championships for college football, NCAA Final Fours, big rock concerts, but I have never experienced anything in this place that so electrified the city.

Sean Payton

The atmosphere in the city that week was like nothing I had ever experienced before. As we got closer to the game, it just grew. I mean, this was a big, big deal. We worked hard to keep the guys focused and to keep their minds on the game. It was an exciting time, and we were all getting into it, but we had a game to play.

Mitch Landrieu

That night at the Superdome really sent out a message to the whole world that New Orleans was coming back. There were so many misperceptions out there about what was happening here. It wasn't just the people in Louisiana who had questioned why we were fixing the Superdome and the Convention Center while people went without housing and schools were still closed. People everywhere were asking if we knew what we were doing.

But the Superdome reopening and the Saints returning and the international media exposure that those two things got were invaluable to us in a million different ways. It let people all over the world know that we were fixing ourselves. We might have a long way to go, but we were heading in the right direction.

Doug Thornton

People started showing up around the Superdome the day before the game. They were just that excited. They wanted to get back in here and get this started.

Sean Payton

Since a lot of the guys had never played a game there, we went down and we had them walk around the place and get used to the lights and the turf. It was a brand-new turf. It felt like a brand-new stadium. It was just amazing.

Steve Gleason, *safety, New Orleans Saints*

The Friday night before the game, Coach Payton had us practice in the Superdome. We went down there and walked around. It was

Many wondered if the Superdome would ever reopen. *Courtesy: Anthony Sisco*

The dome, soon after the evacuees are finally rescued. *Courtesy: Anthony Sisco*

right: Hosting the Chicago Bears at Tiger Stadium during the 2005 season. *Courtesy: Anthony Sisco*

lower left: Turning things around: Head Coach Sean Payton. *Courtesy: Anthony Sisco*

lower right: Saints general manager Mickey Loomis introduces quarterback Drew Brees to the local media. *Courtesy: Anthony Sisco*

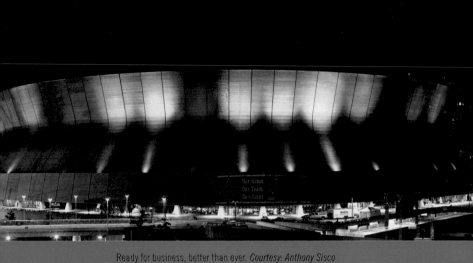

Ready for business, better than ever. *Courtesy: Anthony Sisco*

It's finally time. The Superdome reopens. *Courtesy: Anthony Sisco*

top: Bono and The Edge of U2 join Billy Joe Armstrong of Green Day (center) in "The Saints Are Coming." *Courtesy: Anthony Sisco*

middle: Irma Thomas and Allen Toussaint sing their moving rendition of the national anthem for the Saints' home opener against Atlanta. *Courtesy: Anthony Sisco*

bottom: President George H. W. Bush helps out with the coin toss. *Courtesy: Anthony Sisco*

The Who Dats return to their beloved dome. *Courtesy: Anthony Sisco*

At last, Tom Benson has a reason to boogie. *Courtesy: Anthony Sisco*

Pam Randazza's Black & Gold Sports Shop does brisk business. *Courtesy: H. A. Buchler*

The Saints helped fix many playgrounds just like this one. *Courtesy: Anthony Sisco*

opposite page, top: Roman Harper says, "Not so fast."
Courtesy: Anthony Sisco bottom: Reggie Bush scores his
first touchdown as a Saint. *Courtesy: Anthony Sisco*

opposite page, top: Will Smith takes on Donovan McNabb during Philadelphia's first visit to the Superdome. *Courtesy: Anthony Sisco*

bottom: Devery Henderson heads for the end zone, passing WWL's Kenny Wilkerson (dark suit). *Courtesy: Anthony Sisco*

this page, top: Mark Campbell fights for one more yard. *Courtesy: Anthony Sisco*

bottom: Deuce McAllister outruns the 49ers. *Courtesy: Anthony Sisco*

top: Scott Fujita helps out San Francisco quarterback Alex Smith. *Courtesy: Anthony Sisco*

bottom: Mike Karney scores one of his three touchdowns against Dallas. *Courtesy: Getty Images*

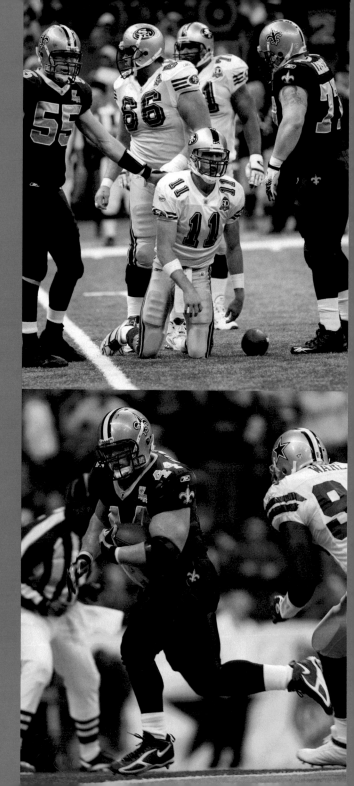

The Saints make life in a FEMA trailer just a little more exciting. *Courtesy: Getty Images*

A fan salutes the Saints' high-powered offense. *Courtesy: Anthony Sisco*

Reggie Bush leads the Who Dat Nation into Times Square. *Courtesy: Planet Hollywood*

Drew Brees says thank you to the fans. *Courtesy: Anthony Sisco*

Deuce McAllister hauls two Eagles defenders down the field. *Courtesy: Anthony Sisco*

Who Dat? Thank you very much. *Courtesy: Anthony Sisco*

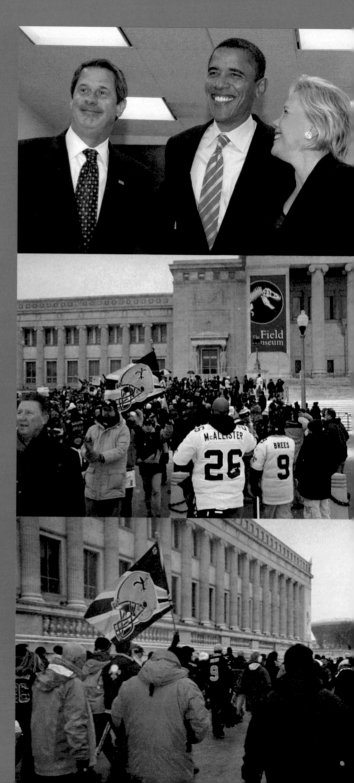

top: Louisiana senators David Vitter *(left)* and Mary Landrieu *(right)* make an NFC Championship bet with Illinois senator Barack Obama *(center)*. *Courtesy: U.S. Senate*

middle: The Who Dat Nation waits in the cold. *Courtesy: Sammy Marten*

bottom: The Who Dat Nation marches on Soldier Field. *Courtesy: Sammy Marten*

Lifelong fan Sammy Marten taunts the Bears in Chicago. *Courtesy: Sammy Marten*

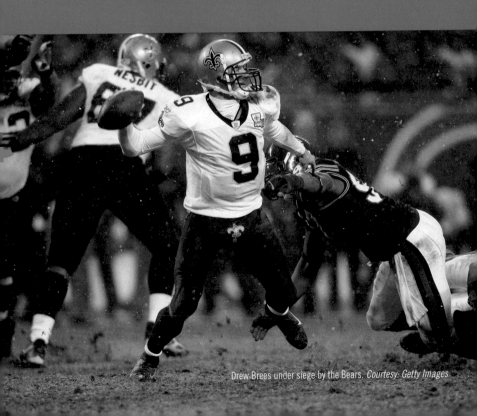

Drew Brees under siege by the Bears. *Courtesy: Getty Images*

The dream is over. *Courtesy: Sammy Marten*

really great for the guys who had played there before to see it again. You know, to work it all out in our heads. He wanted us to deal with the emotional aspects as much as we could so that when we got there Monday night, it could be more about the business of beating those guys.

When we got finished, they dimmed the lights and played a video about Katrina and the dome and the city. It was really moving and inspirational. Here we were, on the floor of the dome, in the dark, watching this video on the giant screens.

I just started crying. When the lights came up, it seemed like everybody was crying. It was good, because now we knew what we had to do. Coach Payton is really smart like that.

Quint Davis

They had this big countdown clock, and we had a stage set up. I knew we'd have a big crowd there, but I wasn't really prepared for how big it was, to be honest. It was like Mardi Gras except that they were all wearing black and gold instead of purple, gold, and green.

Bobby Hebert

It was like some kind of religious pilgrimage or something. The Saints and the Falcons, that's a big rivalry around here. But there wasn't any trash-talking about the Falcons. It was like the game wasn't all that important. It was something so much more going on.

Quint Davis

Leading up to the big event, we had really great local music all day. The Rebirth Brass Band was playing. It just felt so good.

Doug Thornton

I walked around the Superdome that day. The crowd was so thick. There were so many people. And everybody was feeling great. It was very emotional. And the people were so nice. I'm not a celebrity, but I guess people had seen me on TV at press conferences and things like that. I had so many walk up to me and just grab my hand and say, "Thank you, thank you."

I knew that what we had done to get the Superdome back was important. Everybody involved in getting the dome open knew how hard we had worked, but it was special to know that the people knew, too.

Sammy Marten

There's like twenty minutes left before the doors open. I haven't seen my brothers and I don't have a ticket and I am thinking about where I can go watch the game. And, honestly, I have to use the bathroom, too. But the crowd is so thick that I couldn't really go anywhere.

Anyway, right before the doors are going to open, these guys next to me start talking about how their buddy hasn't shown up and how they aren't going to wait for him. A ticket! So, I start telling them how my brother was supposed to meet me here with my ticket, which was total BS.

So we start trash-talking them both, and eventually they get around to telling me I could have their spare if this guy doesn't show up. I'm praying he doesn't, and I keep pretending to be calling my brother, but: "He ain't answering." That clock is down to like one minute and everybody starts inching forward and they finally say, "Screw it. Here, dude." And they hand me the ticket. Literally, as soon as they put the ticket in my hand, the clock hits zero and the confetti starts falling. It was like some wild dream or a movie. I felt like Charlie at the chocolate factory.

Ken Trahan, *manager, Saints Hall of Fame*

The Saints have always brought people together and unified us. Maybe that can be said of all sports teams, but it was never more so than that day at the Superdome. It didn't matter if you were rich or poor or black or white or what religion you were. We were all just Saints fans.

Everybody here had lost something in Katrina, a house or a business or a friend or a loved one. We all lost something. And so we all came together then and shared this really special moment. It was a shared healing.

Dave Dixon

I actually got caught up in the crowd. I had gone to meet one of my sons, and I couldn't get through the crowds. There were just so many people waiting to get in. Any other time I might have been in a hurry, but I really enjoyed working my way through the crowd and seeing it all.

Forget the game and all of the hoopla and the TV networks and the rock concerts. This return has a very special meaning to us. It was something so much more pure. We as a people came together and fixed things. We put something back together. It was a perfect example of the indomitability of the human spirit—*indomitability*!

Doug Thornton

Here were all of these people, so happy, in the exact same spot where there had been so much misery before. I mean standing, literally, in the exact same spot.

In the days after Katrina, after we'd gotten through the misery of waiting it out in the dome, I had watched all those people being bused out and taken out by helicopter. I remember at the time I thought, "We will never see these people again. They're gone." But that night, right before we opened the doors, I know I saw a few of those same faces. They had come back.

As the giant countdown clock struck zero, with black and gold confetti raining down, the doors of the Louisiana Superdome swung open and the faithful returned. Cheering triumphantly and chanting "Who Dat? Who Dat? Who Dat say they gonna beat dem Saints?" 70,003 of the faithful came marching in. It was once again their home. This was their team. And there had been so many saints.

TEARS AND CHEERS

JANUARY 8, 1815, stands as one of the grandest and most glorious days in the history of New Orleans. Forces under the command of General Andrew Jackson defied incredible odds and routed the mighty, redcoat-clad British Army at the Battle of New Orleans. Federal troops and locals pitched in and saved the city from an uncertain future. Perhaps more important than the battle itself, the people of the city had decided to stand up and fight. They themselves saved the city. The day was theirs as much as Jackson's.

On September 25, 2006, almost 200 years later, forces under the command of Coach Sean Payton defied incredible odds and routed the mighty, red jersey–clad Atlanta Falcons. This day, too, will stand as one of the grandest and most glorious days in the history of New Orleans. Just by being able to host the game, the people of New Orleans had again shown the world that they were willing to stand up and fight.

The game drew the highest ratings in the history of ESPN. It was the highest-rated program on television that night on any network, broadcast or cable. In America alone, almost eleven million homes had at least one television tuned to the game. Many networks around the globe—networks that don't usually broadcast American football—carried the game.

And so, with a capacity crowd inside the Superdome, thousands more outside, and a worldwide audience glued to their television sets, New Orleans picked itself up, walked up to the line of scrimmage, and got back in the game. In a pregame show to kick it all off, super bands Green Day and U2 rocked the dome with a soaring anthem, "The Saints Are Coming." And indeed they were.

Sean Payton, *head coach, New Orleans Saints*

We had worked real hard to come into the Superdome 2–0, and we had worked real hard to keep the guys focused on the game and the Falcons. I'm all about preparation, and I felt we were ready.

Now, usually everybody is at the stadium and suited up about two hours before the game, at least two hours before. This is my first big game as a head coach. We have all of this hoopla going on, and we're working real hard to stay focused. Then, all of a sudden, I find out Drew Brees isn't here yet. We had made sure that everybody knew how to get to the Superdome and where to park, and so I just kept thinking, where's Drew? It gets down to like ninety minutes before kickoff, and my quarterback isn't even in the stadium.

Drew Brees, *quarterback, New Orleans Saints*

Of course I knew where the Superdome was and how to get there, but the crowds were just so big all around that part of downtown; I had trouble driving through them. Whole streets were blocked off, and people were tailgating everywhere. It was crazy. Finally I told a police officer who I was. He knew where I had to go, and he escorted me to the entrance.

Sean Payton

Then, when Drew got to the Superdome, he had trouble getting his vehicle into the entrance of the parking garage. He has a truck with these two big antennas or something sticking up. Well, when he tried to go through the entrance, they were too high and they bent. I'm not sure exactly what he did or how he got his truck in there, but he finally got in and started getting ready.

Doug Thornton, *general manager, Superdome*

I looked around, and it was just hard to believe. Here we all were, right back in the Superdome. It was full, and it was exciting.

Dave Dixon, *"Father of the Superdome"*

My God, it was really something. All these people had worked so hard to get this wonderful place open again, and now here it was, full of people and full of energy. I saw Doug Thornton, and I gave him a big hug. "You did it," I said.

And he said, "No, we did it," meaning everybody, not just the two of us, but everybody: Tim Coulon of the stadium commission, the contractors, the workers, the Saints, the NFL, the state, the governor, Mitch Landrieu, everybody. It was very emotional for everybody. I had tears in my eyes.

Doug Thornton

Yeah, I was tearing up a bit, too. A lot of people were.

Mickey Loomis, *general manager, New Orleans Saints*

It's pretty gratifying that we could have that kind of an impact. I was with the Seattle Seahawks when they had the first play-off game in franchise history. I had experienced some big firsts, but nothing like that night. It was indescribable. I've been on the sidelines for Super Bowls. They're incredible. But what was going on in the dome that night was tenfold that.

Mitch Landrieu, *lieutenant governor, Louisiana*

The feeling that night from the governor on down to the team, the fans and even the guys selling beer and popcorn was magnificent. That we could all even be here was just astonishing. It was a real source of pride for everyone. We had hosted Super Bowls before, and it was like this was ours. Maybe this was bigger than if we had been in the Super Bowl.

Quint Davis, *founder and producer, New Orleans Jazz & Heritage Festival*

There was electricity in the air. I mean, really, it was electric. I was standing next to the producer of the Grammy Awards. I reached over to put my hand on his shoulder, and when I touched him there was a snap, a spark. It wasn't static. It was something in the air.

Drew Brees

I don't really know how to describe it, but there was something really special going on in there. You could feel it during warm-ups. You could just feel it.

Will Smith, *defensive end, New Orleans Saints*

I've never heard the crowd be that loud during warm-ups. It was louder in warm-ups than it ever was during some games.

Scott Fujita, *linebacker, New Orleans Saints*

I had been involved in play-off games and a few big games here and there, but never anything like this. We all knew the significance, but being there just overwhelmed us with emotion.

Joe Horn, *wide receiver, New Orleans Saints*

All through warm-ups, I kept looking at the people whenever I had the chance. Man, I was looking at their eyes. I knew what they were thinking. I knew what they were feeling. "This game is to let everybody know we're back. So, after this game, no matter if the Saints win or lose, our team is back in New Orleans and here to stay."

That was what people felt, and I knew it. It was old people and young people, everybody, the entire city of New Orleans, the whole Gulf South, wherever the fans were that night all over the country.

Drew Brees

If we hadn't realized it already, it was during warm-ups that we truly understood that this was so much bigger than just us as a team and our season. This was about so many people, many more people than maybe we even could understand. It transcended the game of football.

Kenny Wilkerson, *sideline reporter, WWL Radio*

Way back when I first started covering the Saints, I was helping my brother, who was also in the media. I would help him get team interviews. He was in another town, and I could do interviews for him here. But it was really just about getting a press pass, you know, to get in for free. Being honest, it was really about getting into the games.

I've been lucky and have made a great career since WWL gave me this opportunity to be the sideline reporter for the Saints radio network. I knew the first time I was on the field that this was what I was meant to be doing, that this was my calling.

I've been on the sidelines for so many games. I don't really know how many. But this one, this one was special. I knew it would be, but I never imagined it could be as moving and emotional as it was. And I'm talking about before the game even started. I have covered a bunch of Super Bowls, and the biggest moments in those games didn't have the drama and emotion and exhilaration that was going on here.

Paul Boudreaux, *director, American Aquaculture Association*

Something that most fans don't realize is that the majority of the concession stands in the dome are run by nonprofit groups. I'm the president and director of a group, the American Aquaculture Association, that has been involved with fund-raising through concession stands for several seasons. Other groups that participate are high school bands, dance teams, beta clubs, and so on.

Our commission for the Monday night game against the Falcons alone was more than the amount we earned *for the entire 2004 season.* The fans deserve to know that out of every dollar they pay for concessions about ten cents goes to local charities. That may take a little sting out of paying $6 for a beer.

Joe Horn

We were in the locker room, and it was time to take the field. It was that time, you know? And so as soon as I walked out of the locker room and started down that hallway, I saw what was happening and could feel the energy from the people.

And then, as players, we waited in the tunnel to come out. The field was right in front of us. The music was playing and all, and I just started crying, weeping. I was crying like a baby. And I knew in my heart—and this is the honest-to-God truth—I'd rather die and give my last breath out on that football field than walk out of there a loser. That's how I felt coming out of that tunnel. I was ready to die. That game, if I had to take a hit and have my knees blown out, end my career and never play another game of football, I'd have done it that night against the Falcons.

Mike Karney, *fullback, New Orleans Saints*

I was crying like a baby out there. A lot of us were. I was just so happy for the fans and for the people of the city.

Marques Colston, *wide receiver, New Orleans Saints*

It was crazy. I felt the stadium moving.

Mickey Loomis

I had tears in my eyes, sure. I don't think there was a dry eye in the place. Maybe on the Falcons' bench there were a couple, but I bet even Jim Mora had some. After all, his dad had coached the Saints in here. It had to be special to him.

Jim Mora, *head coach, Atlanta Falcons*

It reminded me of the early '90s and the late '80s. Late in the game I heard a little "Who Dat." It's a special place. These people are special, resilient, tough, and proud of their city, proud of their football team. I think it really showed. If you have spent any time here, you understand why this is home and they love it here.

Reggie Bush, *running back, New Orleans Saints*

It was my first big home game, and it was Monday Night Football, but I knew, we all knew, that we were playing this game not just for these people here, but also for the thousands of people who lost their lives in Katrina. It was unlike any game I had ever played. Just coming onto that field was unlike anything I had ever felt before.

Scott Fujita, *linebacker, New Orleans Saints*

There was just no chance that the Falcons were going to win that game. We just weren't going to let that happen. We felt that way coming in.

Coach Payton had told us way back in training camp, "If you guys can come into that game 2–0, that place is going to be rocking, and there is no way any team can stop us." And that sentiment had just grown and grown as the game got closer and closer. And now it was here, and there was just no way that the Falcons or anybody else was going to beat us.

Quint Davis

Like I said, I had kind of insisted that Irma Thomas and Allen Toussaint sing the national anthem. The league and the network wanted it to be big, but I said, "No, just Irma signing and Allen at the piano." So that's what it was, and it was beautiful, just fantastic. I think it was just what our people needed. Green Day and U2, that was amazing and terrific and all, but this was something for us.

Steve Gleason, *safety, New Orleans Saints*

As soon as Irma Thomas starting singing the national anthem, I was on. I was looking over at the Falcons' bench, thinking: you guys have *no idea* what you're in for.

Dave Dixon

At football games, some people sing along with the national anthem, but not everybody. That night in the Superdome, *everybody* was singing, with tears streaming down their faces. It was just beautiful.

George Bush Sr. was there to do the coin toss to start the game. When I had pitched Governor McKeithen on the whole idea of building a domed stadium, I'd said that one day a president would be nominated in it. Bush was that president.

George H. W. Bush, *former president of the United States*

There was a certain nostalgia when I went back for the coin toss. I remembered very well getting the nomination right there. It made it more personal for me.

The Superdome was really savaged in a lot of ways. I went into one office upstairs and was really distraught at the wanton destruction. But it came back. Those people in charge did something noble. It gave hope and brought the city alive, although it was coming alive anyway. I'm not one who was pessimistic about New Orleans's future. And then the Saints came along and had a good year—particularly with my "cousin" Reggie Bush in there.

Mikey Loomis

We'd all been collectively holding our breath for months. When the kickoff finally came, I think we all finally exhaled. Now we had a game to play.

Kenny Wilkerson

On the Falcons' very first possession, the Saints really stalled Michael Vick and the offense, and that was a real compliment to our defensive guys. Scott Fujita sacked Vick, and so the Falcons had to punt from their own thirty-five-yard line.

So, Michael Koenen is back to punt, and Steve Gleason gets in there—and he gets a piece of the ball!

Steve Gleason

I was playing a stunt kind of thing, and so it had to be timed just right. I had my arms out and my palms out and I could feel that ball on my hands. I didn't have any idea that I was going to block it until I felt it on my hands. I had blocked punts before, but you never know. Once I felt it, I wasn't sure if I had gotten all of it or just some of it. I didn't know where it had gone, whether it went backwards or forwards or what. I just had my head down and my hands got it.

Kenny Wilkerson

The ball starts tumbling back toward the end zone. Curtis Deloatch falls on it, and the Saints have a touchdown.

I scream. The sideline is going crazy. All the players are going nuts, and the crowd, well, I wear a headset during the game. That's how I know what they're telling me to do in the broadcast booth. Normally, I can't even hear the crowd. Well, I could hear them after that play. It was that loud. I have never heard anything like that in the Superdome, ever.

Quint Davis

Curtis Deloatch, God bless him, he fell on the ball, and it was a touchdown. I thought, oh man, this is for real. This is really happening.

I started screaming, "Touchdown! Touchdown!" And I'm not sure when, but I grabbed the shirt of my friend standing next to me. I grabbed it with both hands, and I was so excited that I ripped a big hole in it. The man had to go the rest of the game with a big hole in his shirt. I don't think he cared. I sure didn't. Not tonight.

Sammy Marten, *fan*

When they blocked that punt, I shouted so much that I lost my voice. Really, it was gone. I still shouted and all but the next day I couldn't talk.

Steve Gleason

When I looked up and saw the celebration in the end zone, I just ran over there and got down on the turf. The roar was just like nothing I have ever heard before. In that moment, I really, honestly felt like I was up in the stands. It was like I was running through the stadium with the fans.

I remember looking up at their faces, really looking at them.

You don't know those people. You don't know who they are. But I looked them in the face at that moment and thought, I know, brother. I know.

I said to myself, "Well, this is it. This is that moment. This is the rebirth of this team and this city." I am so blessed to have been a part of it.

Bobby Hebert, *former quarterback, New Orleans Saints*

We aren't supposed to be cheering in the press box, but a lot of the media guys were. At first, the Atlanta media seemed like they didn't like it, but I think they knew how big this was. Eventually I saw most of them smiling. Maybe they thought it was funny because we weren't being "professionals," but I think they thought it was good.

Mickey Loomis

The blocked punt and the touchdown, I mean, you just can't script that stuff. If you wrote it in a movie, you wouldn't believe it.

Ken Trahan, *manager, Saints Hall of Fame*

Without a doubt, for me, the most important play of the entire season was that blocked punt and the touchdown. You can point to it and say, "That's where it all really came together." You knew right then that these guys could play and that this team was special. It was a turning point for the team, and the city.

Kenny Wilkerson

That play took the wind out of the Falcons. Our defense was playing better than they had expected. Anytime you have a kick blocked like that and then the other team gets a touchdown, it's a letdown. And then with the crowd being so into it and so loud, the emotion of the game just went in the Saints' favor. You could just tell from then on that this was the Saints' night.

Reggie Bush

After that game, we knew we had a real football team. We knew we could make a push for the Super Bowl.

Scott Fujita

I really have to take my hat off to the defensive line. They did such a great job of containing Michael Vick and keeping the pressure on the Falcons all night.

Sean Payton

I was real proud of our team. I had been concerned at the outset that we might be too excited to focus. That was my real concern. But they did well. They handled a very emotional situation very well. We had some good breaks early, and the team played well.

I knew I didn't have to worry about the team's energy dropping in the second half. The crowd wouldn't let that happen, wouldn't let us do that. Something that powerful can mean the difference between winning and losing.

Sammy Marten

It was a blowout. After that blocked punt, all the momentum went our way. When the final seconds ticked down in the fourth quarter, I looked up at the scoreboard and saw the final score was 23–3. I just lost it. Everyone around me was screaming and crying. Nobody wanted to leave. Everybody just stayed chanting "Who Dat!" and dancing in their seats. It was wild.

Anthony Canatella, *deputy superintendent, New Orleans Police Department*

When they won the Atlanta game, I think the people just let it all out. All of the frustrations and emotions just came pouring out. For all that time we'd been holding it in. The team coming back was some people's last hope. It's their identity here. From my perspective, from what I saw on the streets, if the team had not come back, I don't know what would have happened to all of that pent-up energy. More than likely it would have been bad; it might have come out in bad ways. Instead, it was good for the city.

Kenny Wilkerson

That win that night was the biggest win ever for the team up to that point, and that includes beating the Rams in their first play-off win. The fans stayed and were celebrating long after the game was over.

Sean Payton was going around high-fiving everyone, and the players were enjoying it. It was incredible. It was like they had won the Super Bowl. I hate to keep comparing it to that, but in the NFL that's the highest point, the biggest thing you can point to. If there were something higher on the scale, this would still be higher than that.

Really kind of amazing, too, was Tom Benson out there with his umbrella, dancing. He hadn't done that in a long, long time. Remember, this time last year the fans at Tiger stadium were pretty disgruntled and confused, and, rightly or wrongly, a lot of that got directed at him. Now, here he is doing his Benson Boogie with his umbrella with a second line of Saintsations girls right behind him. The fans were cheering him, too. It was like a lovefest.

Scott Fujita

Every year, NFL Films does a highlight film of every team in the league. They had a camera in the locker room after that game. When you watch it you can see what it meant to us. The camera goes around, and you see tears on the faces of a lot of the players and the coaches and some of the upper-management people. It is just unbelievable. I still watch it, and it brings it all right back.

Sean Payton

There were a lot of our guys who did enough out on that field to earn the game ball that night. So many guys could have gotten it, but our choice was unanimous. We gave that game ball to the fans. We awarded it to them. They had earned it. That game was for them. That night was for them.

George H. W. Bush

I think sports has a way of rallying people from all walks of life. Almost everyone I know has a sports team they favor. And for this team—which had not been so heroic in the past—to come back and look so good was just amazing. The mood in the city the day of the opening game was just fantastic. You could feel the excitement in the air that night. A lot of that feeling was because of the team, but it was also because New Orleans was back! New Orleans was not going to stay downtrodden. New Orleans was not going to be beaten.

12

AIN'TS NO MORE

FOR MOST FANS, just seeing their beloved Saints come out of the tunnel and onto the field to start the game would have made 2006 a season to remember. Beating the Falcons had been the cherries on everyone's jubilee. As the city and the team woke up after what had been an epic celebration, they realized something. They were 3–0. They had already matched the sum total of the previous season's wins.

Something good was happening, and not just on the field. Good things began happening in the streets and on the playgrounds all around New Orleans. At long last, the city buzzed again. It had found its beat and got back in rhythm.

The Saints and the fans had traveled together on a very special journey. It had brought them, as one, to the mountaintop, and they had seen the Promised Land. They had forged the most unique bond ever in sports between a team and its home. In the coming weeks, over hills and through valleys, they would work together to make 2006 the most special of times.

Sammy Marten, *fan*

I was just so glad that they had come home. The Superdome was back and the Saints were back and you felt like New Orleans was coming back. Man, that was amazing, fantastic. Beating Atlanta like they did, the Saints made you think maybe there's more. Maybe we had us a team here.

Pam Randazza, *owner, Black & Gold Sports Shop*

Before that game against Atlanta, the people were just thinking, let's get them home and have fun. We really hadn't talked much about the season at all. Now we were talking about it a lot. The Saints really looked pretty good now; they were 3–0, which nobody had expected.

Anthony Canatella, *deputy superintendent, New Orleans Police Department*

I hadn't even thought that they could be back in the Superdome, at all. It wasn't too long ago that I thought that they were gone for good. And let me tell you, I wasn't the only one around here who felt that way. It had never really crossed my mind that they might actually be *good*, but they really played well against Atlanta. I thought, hmm, maybe these guys might have themselves a pretty good season. And by a good season, I mean like a few wins. A few wins, that's all.

Drew Brees, *quarterback, New Orleans Saints*

I think a lot of people probably doubted us even after we were 2–0. They thought we hadn't really played against anybody big, and Atlanta is a very good football team, so "Let's see how you stack up." I think we showed people that we really do stack up.

Kenny Wilkerson, *sideline reporter, WWL Radio*

In training camp they had looked like a team that maybe would be okay. You know, maybe they might go 8–8 or something like that. The Atlanta game and all that went on there had been very emotional, but now they had to play Carolina.

Next up for the Saints were the Carolina Panthers and their Cajun quarterback, Jake Delhomme, himself a former Saint. Jake and the Panthers had been to the Super Bowl before, and many experts were predicting they would again in 2006.

The Panthers had been kind and congenial hosts to the Saints in the wake of Hurricane Katrina. The Saints won their 2005 season opener in Charlotte, 23–20. But that bit of southern hospitality was not repeated when the Saints paid a return visit on the first day of October 2006.

In a game that had produced only 10 total points through the first three quarters, 29 more would be added in the fourth as both teams piled on the offensive yardage. In the end, Carolina would serve New Orleans its first loss of the season, 21–18. While the Saints lost, the game was within reach until the very end. A loss is a loss, but they had shown that they could play with the best in the league.

Sean Payton, *head coach, New Orleans Saints*

I think we all came away frustrated because we didn't win the football game. We just weren't happy about going there and giving a good effort and getting a three-point loss. That's what we play for and that's how we're measured, so I think it was just that.

In the early part of the schedule, you have to keep the emphasis on improving, because I still believe that the minute you stop that hurts your team. There were a lot of little things that all these players and coaches wanted to look at and maybe do differently and then move on.

Joe Horn, *wide receiver, New Orleans Saints*

During the game in Carolina, I caught my 500th pass, which was great, but I would rather have won the game. That's what I am here for. Mr. Benson came by the locker room and said some really nice things. I appreciated that very much. I was hoping that we would have a lot more to celebrate as the season went on.

Kenny Wilkerson

In the Carolina game, I think you saw that "never say die" mentality that they had in Green Bay. Until the final whistle blew, they were in there fighting. It was thrilling and down to the last second and all the things you want it to be, except a win.

By this point in the season, I think everybody was also taking notice of Marques Colston. He had looked pretty good in training camp and then better in the first few games, but now he looked like a star. Against Carolina he caught 5 passes for 132 yards, including that touchdown. He was attracting a lot of attention. The guys covering other teams were starting to ask, "Who is this Colston kid?"

Drew Brees

In training camp Marques was just sort of one of the guys, you know? I don't think he really started to stand out until at least halfway through camp, but his game just continued to elevate each week.

As we got into the season, you started to realize, "Wow! This guy is something special."

It was a process though, a brutal process. It's not something that happens overnight.

Pam Randazza

Marques Colston caught us by surprise. For jerseys, we stock the big names and a few others, but generally most people want Drew, Reggie, and Deuce. We can special-order anybody, but we don't really have them in the store. But I'll tell you, all of a sudden people started asking for Marques Colston jerseys. "I want Marques Colston. My son wants Marques Colston."

So, I get on the phone to my supplier and I tell them, "I want Marques Colston." We started selling a lot of his jerseys. Who would have thought that? But he was good, and that's what sells. If you do well, your jersey sells.

As merchandise flew off the shelves, tickets were harder and harder to come by, too. The Saints were forced to address a concern that had never presented itself before. With the team's first-ever sellout season, how could fans who wanted tickets safely find those who might have tickets to spare? A new system had to be found.

Mike Stanfield, *vice president, ticket and suite sales, New Orleans Saints*

Fans could log onto neworleanssaints.com and click onto Ticket Exchange. There they could find a listing of all the games for which our season-ticket holders have listed tickets for sale. The feedback we received was that this service was a tremendous opportunity for our season-ticket holders who were unable to attend a game. It was safe and affordable for both the buyers and sellers.

Kenny Wilkerson

I wanted to see how the team would react to losing their first game. The Saints had been there before in the past: a bunch of wins right at the start of the season and then they lose and the whole thing collapses. So, I wanted to see how they were in practice getting ready for Tampa Bay. To their credit, it was just back to business as usual.

Steve Gleason, *safety, New Orleans Saints*

Losing is part of the game. You want to win every time, but in reality you probably are going to lose a few. This is a really tough league now. There aren't really any pushovers. Everybody loses one here and there, so you have to take a loss and move on and get ready. The important thing is to not give up. We didn't give up in Green Bay, and we were fighting right to the wire in Carolina, too. We just didn't win, that's all. Now, here comes Tampa and it's a new game and we need to just play that one now.

In front of a sellout crowd at the Superdome, the Saints pirated a 24–21 win from the Tampa Bay Buccaneers in week five.

If the Superdome turf had seemed like a welcome mat to the Bucs, it was pulled out from under their feet in stunning fashion. Reggie Bush hauled down a Josh Bidwell punt and electrified the faithful with a stunning 65-yard return for his first touchdown as a Saint. Chants of "REGGIE! REGGIE! REGGIE!" filled the Superdome. If anyone still had doubts about the first-round draft pick, his numbers against Tampa should have erased them. His 161 total yards included 63 receiving yards, 23 yards gained on the ground, and 75 via punt returns.

Adding to the growing offensive powerhouse, Deuce McAllister ground out an impressive 123 yards while Drew Brees completed 21 of his 33 passes for 171 yards. The Saints record improved to 4–1, keeping them in control of the NFC South.

Reggie Bush, *running back, New Orleans Saints*

That touchdown is right up there with some of the biggest touchdowns I've scored. Obviously this one was even more special because it was the game winner for us. It was a blessing to be able to do that. It was huge for us.

Kenny Wilkerson

For all the hype, Reggie still hadn't scored until then, so that was big for the team and a big relief for him, I'm sure. You know, finally!

Scott Fujita, *linebacker, New Orleans Saints*

I was on the sideline and—I am not lying to you—Mark Simoneau said, "Reggie is going to run this back for a touchdown."

I have no idea what he knew, but he knew something. And then it happened. It had to be a monkey off Reggie's back.

Sean Payton

That was a big win, obviously. It was exciting. I was excited for this team and for the city. The crowd that night had made it very difficult for them on third downs, but from the fans' point of view, the expectations were very high. I hoped that the crowd would continue to generate momentum.

The fans created a great deal of momentum. Too much, almost. Their passion and enthusiasm were forcing the franchise to adapt its operations on the fly. Once again, in a season of historic and unprecedented events, the Saints had to address a new concern. For the first time in history, season-ticket requests outnumbered available seats in the Superdome. The solution was obvious, and a waiting list was created to accommodate future season-ticket holders.

Rita Benson LeBlanc, *owner/executive vice president,*
New Orleans Saints

This process guarantees that those who aim to be season-ticket holders in coming seasons will be able to establish priority now.

We are a regional team, and fans across the Gulf South have rushed to be part of our success. Our fan base stretches across the entire area, and the best way to help the fans who come to our games is to build a list that puts those who were interested first at the top of the line.

After a decisive win over Tampa in week five, New Orleans now hosted Philadelphia. In what would be a preview of things to come, the Saints took the air from the Eagles' wings with a commanding 27–24 win at a now perpetually sold-out Superdome. Joe Horn caught two touchdown passes while Marques Colston notched yet another on his belt.

After their big win over the Eagles, the Saints had a week off to prepare for the Baltimore Ravens, who were returning to the Superdome for the first time since that certain warm, humid August night in 2005 when Hurricane Katrina began inching its way across the Gulf.

Things didn't go New Orleans' way this time, either. Flagged for a staggering ten penalties, the Saints also turned the ball over 5 times, literally handing the Ravens a 35–22 win. Fans were put through a short-lived scare when rookie sensation Reggie Bush sprained his ankle and came out of the game. But Marques Colston continued to shine with six receptions for 163 yards and 2 touchdowns. Joe Horn brought down 5 Drew Brees passes, 1 for a score. Hollywood Joe's touchdown against the Ravens was number 49 in his career as a Saint, setting the team record for most touchdown receptions.

And on one very positive note, fan favorite Michael Lewis returned to the lineup after starting the year on the physically unable to perform list. "Beer Man," as he is known, had joined the team a few years back after carrying beer kegs for a living. Shouts of "Beer Man" could be heard throughout the Superdome as he stepped onto the turf.

Michael Lewis, *kick return specialist, New Orleans Saints*

It felt great to be back. After playing all but two games in 2005, I'd had to sit out the first six this year. It was great coming out, coming out with the crowd in the dome. The bad thing about it is, we didn't come out of it with a win.

Drew Brees

Just look at the stats. The most telling stat of a game every time is turnovers and takeaway ratio. We had 5. We gave them 2 touchdowns as an offense. It hurt. When you do that your chances are not very good.

Sean Payton

The thing we had stressed since the first day of training camp had been eliminating the things that cause you to lose football games, but we did some things like the turnovers and the penalties that got us behind the eight ball, so to speak. We had to get right back to it, identify the mistakes, point them out, and come up with solutions—and then implement them.

The Saints would have a chance to implement those changes and sweep the Buccaneers when they headed down to Tampa for a road game in week eight. The high-powered Saints offense racked up 364 yards while holding on to the ball for more than thirty-seven minutes. Consistently good play by the Saints' defense held Tampa to just 214 total yards. New Orleans completed their sweep of Tampa with a 31–14 win. They flew home with a record of 6–2.

Devery Henderson, *wide receiver, New Orleans Saints*

I had been injured, so I was out for three weeks. I had been out there the week before but I hadn't done too much. I knew I could make plays, I just had to get the confidence back with Drew and the coaches to let them know that I was ready. I went out there and tried to do that.

Will Smith, *defensive end, New Orleans Saints*

Yeah, I had envisioned the success we were having. We knew what we had been up against in 2005 and we knew what we were up against in 2006.

Being that we had played them a couple of weeks before, and that they had a great game against us then, we wanted to show everybody that we could stop them. We wanted to get back on our path defensively. I think we did that.

In any previous season, the two games that followed would have caused doubt for the team and the fans, but this year was different.

In Pittsburgh, the Saints coughed up the ball 3 times, and that proved fatal as the Steelers stole a win, 38–31. Again, the Saints played a very close game against a very good opponent. The Steelers, after all, were the defending Super Bowl champions.

The following week, the Saints hosted the Cincinnati Bengals in the dome. It was a good news, bad news, worse news kind of day. The good news was that Drew

Brees would set a franchise-high mark of 510 yards in a single game, surpassing Aaron Brooks's old record of 441. The bad news was that he completed 3 of his passes to Bengal defenders, and the Saints lost 31–16.

The worse news was that Marques Colston, who by this time was a serious rookie-of-the-year candidate, had to leave the game. Colston was blocking the edge of a Deuce McAllister running play early in the Saints' first offensive series. During the play, the pile of blockers and would-be tacklers rolled into the back of his leg. Colston, a seventh-round draft choice out of Hofstra, had 54 catches for 869 yards, which trailed Carolina's Steve Smith by a single yard for the lead in the NFC, while also owning a team-high 7 touchdown receptions.

Having already swept one division rival, Tampa Bay, the Saints would now travel to Atlanta and complete a sweep of the Falcons with a 31–13 win in the Georgia Dome. Drew Brees burned Atlanta for 349 yards, becoming only the sixth quarterback in NFL history to pass for more than 300 yards in five consecutive games. Seventy-six of those yards came on a touchdown toss to Devery Henderson. The Saints defense held the usually high-flying Falcon offense in check, allowing quarterback Michael Vick only 84 yards in the air. Will Smith had 2 sacks, and Charles Grant had 1.

Week 13 brought the 49ers to the Superdome. The San Francisco team may have been named in honor of the California Gold Rush, but it was Reggie Bush who hit pay dirt that day. By game's end he had rushed for 37 yards and 3 touchdowns while hauling in 9 Brees passes for another 131 yards and his fourth score of the day.

The always-productive Deuce McAllister churned out 136 yards, and, on the other side of the ball, Saints cornerback Mike McKenzie took in 2 of the Saints 3 interceptions of 49ers quarterback Alex Smith, who was also sacked 4 times. The Saints had played an almost flawless sixty minutes of football.

Although the Saints won 34–10, dulling the luster of this golden day was the loss of Joe Horn to a groin injury. As Hollywood Joe Horn walked off the Superdome turf that day, it seemed like a minor incident. Few realized that this record-setting, always-entertaining receiver had played his last game in a Saints uniform.

After twelve outings, the Saints were now 12–4. They were firmly in control of both the NFC South and, remarkably, their own destiny. With the boys in black and gold taking such firm control of their future, New Orleans and the Gulf Coast were taking control of their own as well.

Mitch Landrieu, *lieutenant governor, Louisiana*

By attracting national attention and catching the eye of the nation, the Saints gave us a real opportunity to showcase what we could do. Our economy needs tourists and convention business, and so we were able to let the world see that we were putting things back together here. Every week people saw something completely different from what they had seen in the weeks and months after Hurricane Katrina.

The people here were great, too. While we had enormous, capacity crowds, they were really well behaved. That let us show the convention planners—who really in many cases decide where these events will take place—that the NOPD could handle the crowds. It let them know that we could handle big events.

Having so much of our culture—the French Quarter and our restaurants and our music—highlighted by the media in such a positive way, that got people interested and excited about coming here to visit.

Anthony Canatella

We really didn't have any trouble at the Superdome at all. I mean, really nothing to talk about. Maybe somebody might have a few beers and get a little rowdy, but nothing serious at all. Saints fans, by and large, have always been pretty well behaved, but this year even with as many people as we had every game, they were better behaved than ever.

And in the city, well, crime actually goes down during a Saints game. Everybody is watching the game so they aren't out there to commit crimes. To be honest, I wish the Saints were playing twenty-four hours a day; then we'd have no crime ever.

Michelle Babineaux, *owner, Michaul's Cajun Dance Hall*

After Katrina I had lived in fourteen different places in the first twelve months. I maybe thought about leaving New Orleans for a little bit, but I just decided that this was my home and I wasn't going anywhere. I went back to Venetian Isles and started fixing things up.

And down at my restaurant, I still wasn't open six nights a week like I had been, but I was starting to get some business back. With the Saints doing what they were doing and fans from other cities starting to come here, I started feeling pretty good about things. I felt like, give it time and I'll be okay.

Abbe Garfinkel, *fan*

I had a bit of good luck. Finding contractors had been tough because there just weren't enough workers to help everybody who needed it, but I found one, and he started working on my house. It was going to take a long time because of the historic nature of my house, but at least something was happening.

Right after the storm I had gotten work in Mississippi with one of the companies that helped get people into trailers if they had lost their homes, so that was good. I finished my studies, and then I was able to really get involved. I started work at the Children's Bureau, where we helped children who had been traumatized by seeing a murder or something else horrible. Now we were treating kids who had lived through all of the horrors of Hurricane Katrina. The Children's Bureau is part of the United Way, and the Saints are huge contributors to it, so that was really good.

Roger Gorman, *Children's Hospital*

Many, many Saints help us out here. They come to visit the kids and that has always been fantastic, but this year especially was just remarkable. Nothing was more exciting for the children than when a Saints player came to visit.

Kevin Houser, who is not what you would call famous, has come by often and I think it is as exciting for him as the kids. They just love him, and he'll say "Oh, but I'm just the long snapper." But I think it is really just that these kids get to see and talk with a Saints player.

The Saints have always been good about having some of our children at the games and that is really fantastic, but, of course, not every patient can go. If you walked the halls here during a Saints game, you'd think you were at the Superdome, really. You'd hear cheering and everything. Being in a hospital for a long time can really wear the kids and their families down, so to have that fun and excitement, well, it does wonders for them. We had a lot of patients with Saints decorations in their rooms.

Brian Grenrood, *public relations, Children's Hospital*

FOX 8 asked me to come back to work for them in Mobile, but I had had enough. I didn't go back. I worked cutting trees for the Corps of Engineers for a while and then went to work for Children's Hospital in public relations in May.

Almost every day, somebody would come in trying to make a donation. They would say, "Drew Brees signed a jersey for me, and he said, 'Okay, I'll sign this for you, but only if you do something for me: make a donation to Children's Hospital.'" I can't tell you how many people came in and did that because Drew asked them to.

Kenny Wilkerson

We had a caller to the show, a guy named Steve. He told us about how all the people in his neighborhood were gathering every week out on the neutral ground to watch the games. They all were living in FEMA trailers; one guy got an extension cord, they brought this big TV out to the neutral ground every week and watched the game. These are people, neighbors, who really had never gotten to know each other, and now they were all watching the games together.

Bobby Hebert

They all pitched in and had fun watching the games. The Saints were bringing people together like that. It was really exciting to watch.

Paul Boudreaux, *director, American Aquaculture Association*

My favorite part of doing concessions is interacting with thousands of fans, especially young people. I saw more kids and young people getting into the team than ever before. That whole year was a feeling of euphoria. Everyone thought we could not lose and were going all the way to the big one. The noise level was twice as loud as past seasons also.

Daniel Garroway, *fan, age twelve*

My Saints story has to do with a project I did for school in a social studies contest. It was about the value of a sports franchise to a community, and I used the Saints as a large part of my project to show how valuable the team is to New Orleans, especially since Hurricane Katrina. I won first place at my school, Mary Queen of Peace in

Mandeville, for the economics category, and I was allowed to go to Hammond to compete in the regional competition. I chose the topic because I like the Saints and I think they were very important to the New Orleans recovery efforts after the Hurricane.

Billy Cundiff, *placekicker, New Orleans Saints*

I had joined the team right at Thanksgiving, and so I was just walking into this. I hadn't been here to see it grow and catch on. But it was really amazing how much the people loved this team. I had never experienced anything like it.

My wife and I went to eat at Dickie Brennan's Steak House. I had only been with the Saints for a few weeks at the most, and this guy comes over and says, "Hey, you're Billy Cundiff."

I was like, "Yeah, I am. But how do you know who I am?"

And he was like, "You're a Saint."

He was just thanking me and thanking me for what the team had done. I really hadn't been part of it yet, and I tried to explain that to him, but he just kept thanking me anyway. Trust me, that doesn't go on anywhere else, not that I know of.

Scott Fujita

Everywhere you went in New Orleans, if people recognized you, they would just really get excited. In any other city it's like, "Hey, great game." Or, after a loss, "You guys stink."

Here, even after we would lose a game, people were still happy. Even when we lost those two back to back, same thing. They were just thrilled about it all. My wife and I and most of the players got really into it. These people in New Orleans were just so positive about it all, so positive about life. You couldn't help but feel that, hey, this is really something special. Take it all in.

• • •

If there were any remaining questions about whether or not the Saints were for real, they were answered resoundingly in Dallas, Texas, in a nationally televised Sunday-night showdown with the Cowboys. Both teams entered the game with identical 8–4 records. The Cowboys had manhandled the Saints back in the pre-season, 30–7, and most experts believed that the Saints' fairy tale would finally come to an end.

Head coach Sean Payton would stand opposite his mentor, legendary coach Bill Parcells. Drew Brees was returning to Texas Stadium to play for the first time since quarterbacking his team to the Texas High School Football Championship there. The linebacking Scotts—Fujita and Shanle—were also returning to face their former team, as was kicker Billy Cundiff.

The Cowboys scored first on a 77-yard run by Julius Jones—the only score by either team in the first quarter—but the rest of the night would be all New Orleans. Mike Karney, the Saints' hardworking but unheralded fullback, scored 3 times with a 2-yard run and touchdown receptions of 3 and 6 yards each. Jamal Jones came out from behind the shadows of the more famous receivers to catch a 27-yard touchdown pass.

The first half ended with the saints ahead 21–7. The Cowboys opened the second half with a 24-yard field goal. That was quickly answered by Reggie Bush and Drew Brees as they connected on a 61-yard touchdown pass. Terrell Owens gave the Cowboys their last score of the evening, capping a Dallas drive of 63 yards. Then Brees and company answered right back with a 63-yard drive ending in Karney's third touchdown.

Wanting to close the door on any chance for a late rally by the Cowboys, Sean Payton advised his quarterback to be ready for an onside kick. Brees, always aware and thinking, followed his usual routine of taking off his helmet and returning to the bench to look at overhead photos of the previous drive—that helped conceal the plan. As Brees watched from the bench, kicker Billy Cunduff hit the ball per-fectly, then made a downfield block that allowed Jay Bellamy to recover the ball. Four plays later, Brees found Devery Henderson from 42 yards out to extend the Saints' lead to 25.

Perhaps the Saints could have scored even more on the demoralized Cowboys, but Sean Payton, in deference to his former mentor, called off the attack. In the stands, thousands of Saints fans had made their way to Texas Stadium, far more than the norm at any average road game. As the game wound down, they began to chant "WHO DAT? WHO DAT? WHO DAT SAY DEY GONNA BEAT DEM SAINTS???" And their chanting overwhelmed the silent and stunned Dallas crowd.

13

WHO DAT NATION

THE SAINTS LEFT Dallas victorious. By the time their plane landed at Louis Armstrong Airport in New Orleans, they were beyond a doubt the Cinderella story of 2006. In fact, the story of this team and this city will most likely go down as one of the greatest ever. Not only had the Saints captured the imagination of New Orleans and the Gulf Coast, their following had spread across the country.

For ages, the Dallas Cowboys had been "America's Team." Their famous cheerleaders and the big star on their helmets had a particular resonance with the entire country. Now sportscasters began referring to the Saints as the new "America's Team." They not only represented hope for an area ravaged by the worst natural disaster in our nation's history, they were also getting the job done on the field. America loves a winner, and New Orleans was winning in style.

Following their win in Dallas, the Saints were the number one–ranked offense in the entire NFL, averaging over 100 yards per game on the ground. Drew Brees's passing game was sky-high at 303.5 yards per outing, nearly 30 yards more per game than that of Peyton Manning's highly touted Colts. Brees himself was leading the league in completions, completion percentage, passing yards, touchdowns, and average gain per pass. His quarterback rating of 101.2 was the finest in the league.

On the receiving end of his passes, two rookie sensations were making their mark. Reggie Bush led the NFC with 79 receptions while Marques Colston led all rookie receivers with 917 yards, despite missing most of three games.

On defense, Will Smith had brought down enough quarterbacks to place fifth in the NFL in sacks. The patchwork quilt of a defense the Saints had stitched together ranked twelfth overall and fifth against the pass.

The Saints were on a roll. Fleurs-de-lis began appearing on almost every street in town. Black-and-gold fever had taken over.

Scott Fujita, *linebacker, New Orleans Saints*

Even after the Dallas game, we were all still talking about the fans. The win was great and all, but I think, looking back, the thing I'll remember most are those fans being at that game and so totally taking over the stadium. It was awesome, just awesome.

Drew Brees, *quarterback, New Orleans Saints*

You should have seen how many Saints fans were there from Louisiana, from East Texas. I'm sure we'd been picking up a lot of fans along the way throughout the season, but it was amazing to see so many of them there.

When the game was ending, our fans stuck around and kind of meandered their way down to the front into those first few rows. They were holding up signs and hooting and hollering and doing the "Who Dat?" I had played in that stadium ten years before in high school and had many great memories of it, and those fans gave me another great one.

Mickey Loomis, *general manager, New Orleans Saints*

Our fans, without a doubt, are the best in the league and probably all of sports. They have supported this team through so many years, even when things didn't go the way everybody would have liked. And to have gone through what they've gone through, the disruption in their personal lives, the tragedies, and then to be in Dallas, a road game, and to be so vocal, well, it's just another of those really great memories for myself and the entire organization.

Reggie Bush, *running back, New Orleans Saints*

It's nice to feel loved in your home city and all, but when your fans do like ours did on the road, you just know it's special. You feel wanted even more.

Steve Gleason, *safety, New Orleans Saints*

That was so unique, to have that many of the Who Dats there in Texas. I remember saying to myself, "Take it in. Take it all in. This is another really special moment. Remember this."

Bobby Hebert, *former quarterback, New Orleans Saints*

People all over America follow football, but most places don't have a team. In those places they follow whatever team is on TV or is winning. Well, the Saints had been in some big games this year, and everybody was aware of them.

People love to cheer for the underdog, and New Orleans and the Saints were the ultimate underdogs in the beginning, but now they were winning, too, so it just got bigger. I would be in airports with a Saints shirt on, and people would come up to me and say, "Man, I am just so happy for you guys." They'd say, "I'm from Topeka, and I'm a Saints fan." Everywhere you went, there were Saints fans.

When they beat Dallas, people were calling in and saying that the Saints were the new America's team. Well, I remembered hearing fans of the Red Sox being called the Red Sox Nation, so I said that Saints fans were the Who Dat Nation, and it really caught on from there. Our station, WWL, started calling themselves the home of the Who Dat Nation. We started getting calls from all over the country—Virginia, Ohio, California, Nevada—and people would all say that they were part of the Who Dat Nation.

Pam Randazza, *owner, Black & Gold Sports Shop*

It had just been nonstop all season. We were not only selling a lot of things in the store, but as soon we closed up I had to take care of the orders from the website—we started selling as much online as in the store. We could hardly handle it.

We were getting orders from literally every state—and Canada, especially in the French parts of Canada. We even had orders from France. We had a few from other places, but a lot from France. They wanted the fleur-de-lis gear.

By the time Christmas came, I think everybody in New Orleans must have given somebody else something from the Saints as a gift. It was crazy in here. I had over twenty employees, and we had lines out of the door the entire time we were open. I think we could have stayed open twenty-four hours a day and still had people coming.

My supplier actually ran out of jerseys. The supplier makes so many in each size in either black or white, then I call and say, "Print me this many Drew Brees and this many Reggie Bush," or whomever.

Well, at one point, they said, "Pam, we're out of jerseys."

So I had to get whatever jerseys I could get my hands on until the supplier could make more. That's never happened before.

Scott Fujita

After the games, you have a little time to shower and dress and then you go do interviews with the media. Sometimes you've sort of come down from playing, but I was still pumped, I guess. I was talking to the linebacker Danny Clark, and I said something like, "Wouldn't it be great if we had this kind of support up in New York in two weeks?"

And he was all about it, so we said, "Let's give twenty-five tickets to the first twenty-five fans who show up at the Saints facility." It was just spur of the moment. We didn't think about it that much or really think it through. I told Fletcher Mackel from WDSU what we were going to do to, and then it just caught fire.

Steve Gleason

Man, what I great idea. I was in right away, without a doubt. Everybody wanted in on it. Are you kidding? Reward the fans and get them in New York? It was just brilliant. We ended up offering like fifty tickets, I think.

Kenny Wilkerson, *sideline reporter, WWL Radio*

Well, I could have told them what was going to happen. I think half the city must have jumped in their cars and tried to get out to Airline Drive. I hear there were hundreds of people out there.

Bobby Hebert

After the game, people were calling in. "How can I get those tickets? Are there any left? How many can I get?"

I just told them, "You better hurry, because they aren't going to last long."

By then they were gone, no doubt. People didn't even know how they were going to get to New York, but they were going, that's for sure.

Scott Fujita

It was really just something that we thought of in the moment. We really didn't go talk to anybody in management about *how* to do it. I was just saying to the media guys that we were doing this.

So, there is like one guy at the complex during away games, just sort of taking care of things and answering phones. He starts getting bombarded with people. They're calling and knocking on the door. He had people putting envelopes under the door; it got crazy out there. But this guy, he realizes how crazy this could get, and he takes it on himself to put all of these requests and cards and letters in some kind of order so we could at least be fair about who gets the tickets.

When we did this, we had no idea that many people would want to go. The game is in New York on Christmas Eve. Who would want to be on a plane on Christmas Eve? But we had so many requests come in so fast that the tickets were really spoken for in minutes. We could have given away a hundred times more tickets, and there still would have been more fans wanting to go. I wish we could have given more out. Ultimately me, Danny Clark, Steve Gleason, Charles Grant, Jason Craft, Mike McKenzie, Terrance Melton, Mark Campbell, Mark Simoneau, and Brian Young all gave away tickets.

Mickey Loomis

Sure, maybe we would have liked a little warning so we could have organized things a little better, but I think it being so spontaneous and genuine means more in the long run. It let the players give something back to the fans, and I know that made them feel good.

Drew Brees

I was named NFC Offensive Player of the Week, which is really a great honor. Reggie had been given the same honor a week before. I know it sounds cliché and all, but that really isn't just for me. I'm just the guy they single out, to put one name on it. Awards like that are really for the whole offense, the whole team, every single guy.

Sean Payton, *head coach, New Orleans Saints*

When you win on the road, you really only have only about twelve hours to enjoy it, and then you're back at work getting ready for the next one.

At this point in the season, with three games left, everybody starts to look at all of the play-off scenarios that can take place. We had to look at and work on the team we were playing that week: the Washington Redskins. The rest of it would take care of itself. Nothing's guaranteed. We had nine wins, and we were fighting for our tenth. We had a chance to do something at home for the fans and for ourselves.

For the game against the Redskins, New Orleans had invited international superstar Harry Connick Jr. to sing the national anthem. Connick was born and raised in New Orleans, and in the days and weeks after Katrina, he had helped draw attention to the needs of people in the city. Through concerts and telethons as well as the release of various recordings, he had helped raise vast amounts of money desperately needed to help rebuild his beloved hometown. With Connick in the house, it should have been another storybook day at the dome, but that was not to be.

Thanks to a third-and-goal touchdown from Deuce McAllister and a field goal from John Carney, the Saints stayed in the game until the very end. But the Redskins just brought more to the field that day. Once again, the scoreboard showed a Saints loss, 16–10.

But this loss came with a happy ending. In the crazy, late-season mishmash of play-off probabilities, while losing to the Redskins, the Saints had captured the NFC South title. All that had been needed was a loss by the team's closest challenger, Carolina. The Pittsburgh Steelers took care of that with a 37–3 romp over the Panthers. Although it was the Saints' first division title in the relatively new NFC South, they had won titles in their old division, the NFC West, in 1991 and 2000. Yes, the Saints were going to the play-offs in this most unlikely of seasons.

Scott Fujita

Sure, we were division champs, but we were still disappointed. We could have locked up our first-round bye right then. But however we did it, we had gotten it done, and I know that the fans were really proud of us.

Deuce McAllister, *running back, New Orleans Saints*

For the city and the organization, we were proud to be going to the play-offs and to have won the division, but at the same time we still had to look at this game. How much did we improve? When you go to the play-offs, you have to be on a roll. I knew we had to get our act together or we'd be one and out.

Drew Brees

It was a tremendous honor to win the NFC South, especially if you look at where we were at the start of the season. I think everybody in America had us picked fourth in our division, and now here we are the division champs. I'd say that was a pretty big accomplishment. It was one of our goals, something we had set out to do. Our next goal was to set up home-field advantage.

Sean Payton

I think the good news was that we won the NFC South. You set goals. You come out of training camp, and you play your schedule. This was my first year as a head coach and that maybe made me a little anxious, but one of our goals was to win the division, and we did that with two weeks left in the season.

If you go around the league, ultimately, every team talks about winning the Super Bowl, and I can tell you our team was no different. You play this game to win a championship. The first step is winning the division, which we did. My son Connor was the tee retriever for that game, by the way. I thought he did a pretty good job. He hustled, and he ran better than I thought he would.

Abbe Garfinkel, *fan*

Division champs, can you believe it? I mean really, could you just have imagined it? Okay, so, no crash and burn for Sean Payton, but I did keep his pictures on the refrigerator.

That week, in conjunction with the Saints-Redskins game, wives of the Saints, Redskins, Miami Dolphins, and Denver Broncos gathered in Hammond to help build two new houses for the Ginger Ford Habitat for Humanity. As members of an NFL players' wives organization, Off the Field, the women have sponsored four new homes for Habitat's hurricane recovery program, Operation Home Delivery.

Blair Edwards, *executive director, Ginger Ford Habitat for Humanity*

Not only have these women fully funded four new homes in Hammond, but they came out from cities across the country and truly invested themselves in this community. We could not have been more grateful for their support.

Sammy Marten, *fan*

One of my brothers told me about the wives coming to Hammond to help with Habitat for Humanity. My family knows one of the people who got a house, so that really hit close to home for me. I knew that they had been doing a lot of good stuff down in New Orleans, but knowing that they came out to a little town like Hammond . . . what can I say? Don't get me wrong, I was all excited that they had won the division and all, but this was a big thing to me and to my family and to my hometown. I know my dad would have been real proud to know that his team was here doing something like this. He would have been real proud.

Kenny Wilkerson

Just a few days after the Redskins game, they announced the Pro Bowl selections. From the Saints, Jammal Brown, Will Smith, and Drew Brees would be there to represent the NFC in Honolulu.

Sean Payton

I was excited to see Drew selected to the Pro Bowl. He worked so hard on his rehabilitation. It's amazing to see the commitment he makes every single day to hard work and leading this team. To see him recognized as one of the top quarterbacks in the league was a tribute to the job he's done as a Saint.

And Jammal had put so much hard work into his adjustment, too. He switched from right tackle to left tackle and then made the Pro Bowl in his first year. That's just not easy. I believe he was a big reason why we had the success we had on offense in 2006.

And Will Smith, he'd been a big force for us defensively all season. He was a major part of our improvement on defense and, as a player, he is someone who prepares both on and off the field very diligently every week.

I was real proud of these guys, of our whole team really. I wish they could have all gone to the Pro Bowl.

Drew Brees

That was a tremendous honor. It was one of my personal goals entering the season, and I would not have been selected without the incredible efforts of the guys on my team and what we had been able to accomplish together.

Jammal Brown, *tackle, New Orleans Saints*

It was an honor and a blessing. I'll take some of the credit, but really much of it has to go to my teammates and coaches. If it weren't for the older guys on my team like Jeff Faine, Jamar Nesbit, and Jon Stinchcomb, and all of the time that Coach Marrone put in with me going all the way back to training camp, I wouldn't have made it.

Will Smith, *defensive end, New Orleans Saints*

All of those individual honors are decided by the writers and the voters. Yeah, it's something that every player would like to get, but I would have traded it for a Super Bowl win. Right then, I was more focused on us being the number two seed in the play-offs and getting that bye and the home-field advantage.

Sean Payton

There was still a lot to play for in those last two weeks. The NFC was by no means settled, and a lot could have changed. So we had to shake off the loss to the Redskins, learn from our mistakes and move on. We were going up to New York to face the Giants. They had a good team, and I didn't think we'd have any trouble getting our players' attention.

Drew Brees

Going up to New York, I thought it was extremely important that we get an early lead on the Giants. You have to get up early on them, and we really pride ourselves on starting with a fast tempo. This was do or die for them, because they needed to win both of their last two games. The faster we could get up on them, the better.

The game had been billed as an NFC showdown in the Big Apple, but it turned into a Christmas Eve party for the visiting New Orleans Saints. Earlier in the season, Giants great Tiki Barber had announced his retirement, and this game, his last at home, was to be a showcase for his offensive talents. The programs on sale at the Meadowlands featured his likeness, and the stadium was covered with banners honoring him. However, as they so often are, one legend was supplanted by another: Reggie Bush mowed the Meadowlands for a season-high 126 yards and a touchdown. Deuce McAllister had his own piece of Big Apple pie with 108 yards and a touchdown of his own.

The Giants jumped out to an early 7–0 lead but it was the only time they posed any serious threat to the Saints' end zone. An offensive barrage from New Orleans put the final score at 30–7.

As for Tiki Barber's big Christmas send-off, the Saints' defensive line played the part of Scrooge, allowing the Giants only 142 yards of total offense. They also forced and recovered 2 fumbles and picked off the young Eli Manning for an interception. So complete was the domination by the defense that the Giants didn't take an offensive snap inside of Saints territory for the entire game. Bah humbug, Big Blue! This was a very merry Who Dat Christmas.

Drew Brees

That was a great all-around effort by everybody. Anytime you have two one-hundred-yard rushers like Reggie and Deuce, it's a testament to them and the offensive line. We had great blocking from Mike Karney and some really good downfield blocks by our receivers.

I really loved our aggressive style and our aggressive mentality. That's the mentality we have as an offense. We never let that die, even when we'd built a lead.

Scott Fujita

That was a remarkable game for the guys on defense. That one was really big for us. We just shut them down.

After the game, near the locker rooms I saw some of the people we had given tickets to. That was great, too. They were all saying thank you. I was just like, "No, man. Thank you guys. Merry Christmas."

Abbe Garfinkel

I remember how bleak the holidays were in 2005, when *nothing* good was happening. You're supposed to forget your troubles at this time of year, but we all had so many. Can you imagine what it was like having the holidays in a FEMA trailer? It would have been horrible without them, without the Saints. So many of us were still not in real homes and there were so many problems with this and that, but to see them winning on Christmas Eve was just really special.

Kenny Wilkerson

Even before the game there had been this real feeling of excitement all around town. They had won the division, and they were going to host the play-offs, but the city just cut loose after the New York game. We didn't even know they'd gotten the bye yet.

Bobby Hebert

It was Christmas Eve, and the people calling in were talking about going out to the airport to greet the team. It was cold and there was a little rain and they were calling, saying everybody should go, on Christmas Eve, and wait for the team outside the airport. I thought, man, don't they have somewhere to be on Christmas Eve? But, I guess, for a lot of people Christmas that year meant being in a trailer or on somebody's sofa. So, really, it was a place for them to go to feel good.

Down here, along the Mississippi River, people go on the levees and have those big bonfires to light the way for Papa Noel so he can find the kids. I guess it was like that. The Saints were like Papa Noel or something.

• • •

With the NFC South title in hand, and earning a bye in the play-offs, coupled with the home-field advantage, Sean Payton was faced with a situation never before encountered by a Saints head coach in the entire forty-year history of the franchise: What to do against Carolina in the Superdome on New Year's Eve? Neither a win nor a loss in this final game would change what they had earned. So how would they handle the situation? Do you take a chance on losing your last game before heading into the play-offs, or do you make sure that you don't put key players at risk of injury?

Regardless of the outcome, New Year's Eve 2006 would cap a great year for the Saints and the city.

Sean Payton

We, as a staff, really needed to think about how we would handle this. We still wanted to win every game we lined up for. We had to come up with a plan even though everything had been laid out there in front of us.

Every decision I make is in the best interest of the New Orleans Saints. I knew that we wanted to play well, and so did the Panthers. That game had play-off implications not just for them, but for other teams, too. But my focus had to be on what gives the Saints the best chance to win in the long run, what helps us get to where we need to get to most.

Bobby Hebert

When I was with the Saints, we had won all of those games back in 1987, the strike year, and the last game really didn't matter much. We didn't win the division, though, because the 49ers did. Jim Finks and Coach Mora hinted that maybe they would rest me for that game, but I wanted to play. The money was all different back then, too. I didn't get as much base salary as they do now, and I had big bonus clauses if I started this many games or that many games. If I didn't start that game, it was going to cost me, like, $200,000. I told Dave Wilson, "Look, I am going on that field at the start of the game. I'll hand off to Dalton Hilliard or something like that, and then come out. But don't you dare try and go out on that field. Go hide or lose your helmet or something and I'll give you $50,000."

Coach Mora let me start so I didn't have to worry about it. Things have all changed now, and so Drew didn't have to think about stuff like that. I know that never was on Coach Payton's mind, either. You know, times have changed.

Kenny Wilkerson

Honestly, nobody knew exactly what they were going to do. You know, who was going to play and for how long, that sort of thing.

Reggie Bush

I didn't want to come out. I want to be in there all game, every game. I went into that game like every guy on the team, thinking, I am playing the whole four quarters.

Kenny Wilkerson

By game time, we knew that Drew was going to start, and so was Reggie. They had deactivated Deuce and Fred Thomas, Will Smith, Terrance Copper. And, of course, Joe Horn was not really 100%, so he was out, too.

Abbe Garfinkel

So out comes Drew Brees to start the game, and I start screaming at the TV, "Payton, what the hell are you doing? Don't get Drew hurt, you idiot."

And then Drew fumbles and has to get that back. I thought I was going to lose my mind. If Sean Payton had been anywhere near me, I don't know what I would have done to him.

Kenny Wilkerson

So here you go, Drew fumbles and has to jump on it. That's *exactly* the thing he did when he got his shoulder injury, so I'm thinking, this just can't be. But he gets up and sort of grins and lines up again.

Everybody was thinking, okay, Coach, you made your point. Now get him out of there before something bad happens.

They drive down, and Reggie scores from 1 yard out. Okay, great, now we've seen Drew and Reggie, so tell them to go take a seat. Good job.

Then Carolina goes right down the field, and Jake Delhomme throws a touchdown to Steve Smith. So it's 7–7, and they kick off to us.

Michael Lewis really rips a great kickoff return for like 51 yards, and then here comes Brees again. I'm like, "What can you possibly be thinking, Payton?"

Bobby Hebert

All I kept saying was, "Man, you guys are crazy."

Abbe Garfinkel

So, I'm thinking, all right, you let 'em score. Great. Now take 'em out. But, here he comes again. I can't repeat what I was screaming. I'm surprised the neighbors didn't call the police. I'm thinking, they have got be nuts. That priss, that little priss. I could just see those lips getting tighter and tighter.

Kenny Wilkerson

On first down, Drew hits Mike Karney for eight yards, and Payton calls time out. Brees turns and starts trotting toward the sidelines and taking off his helmet. Well, everybody knew he was coming out and they started cheering and he got a standing ovation. The whole Superdome was chanting, "MVP! MVP! MVP!!"

Drew Brees

It was one of those things where you have to savor the moment a little bit. Coach Payton had kind of planned it: I would go in and get a couple of reps just to stay sharp and then come out. I didn't want to make a big deal out of it, but it really turned out to be a special moment. For me, maybe, it was like all of the things from the season culminating in one moment.

Bobby Hebert

It was so good to see him get that kind of ovation from the crowd, you know? It was like they were all saying, "Thank you."

Mickey Loomis

Drew was really the guy who got us rolling at the very beginning. He had believed in us and had been a leader, so it was just great to see the fans treat him so nicely.

Steve Gleason

Way back, Drew had been the guy who stepped up, and we had all really followed him. He was the leader, so every guy on the team cheered when he came off. We were cheering for him and for us and for what we had all done. It wasn't just like "Oh, hey, great job, Drew." That moment was for everything we had done together as a team.

Abbe Garfinkel

We all stood up and cheered and applauded, right there in the trailer. "Yes! Yes! Thank you!"

Kenny Wilkerson

The real highlight of the day—at least for me and I think for a lot of people—was Fred McAfee getting a touchdown. The guy has been in the league for a really long time, and they had let him go and then brought him back. If you know Fred, you know the guy is always smiling. He really hasn't been a running back in years, and that's what he came in as. He's really been a special-teams guy. When he got the ball and scored, you could just see smiles everywhere.

Drew Brees

Freddie Mac is one of the best teammates that I have ever had and the type of guy where I relished every moment that I got to spend with him. I think his attitude is second to none. He loves the game of football. He added a lot to our team production-wise on special teams and deserves every bit of credit. Guys like Fred are what separate the championship teams from the average teams. Fred McAfee makes it fun to go to work every day.

Sean Payton

There is a guy who gave us whatever we asked of him, 100%, every time. We had made roster moves and had to let him go and then get him back a few times in 2006. He never complained.

I was real glad that I had the opportunity to call his number and let him get one, a touchdown. I think Fred is still carrying that ball around with him. I mean, right now. If you bump into Fred somewhere, don't be surprised if he's carrying that ball with him.

Fred McAfee, *running back, New Orleans Saints*

It felt real good to get my number called and to be able to score. It was really special for me, really special. I won't ever forget it, never.

I was the only guy who had played on all three Saints division championship teams. I had been there in 1991 with Coach Mora and in 2000 with Jim Haslett and now with Coach Payton. I'm just so glad I had those opportunities. Now, I just kept telling myself, you gotta be on the Saints team that wins the Super Bowl, and I felt like if we could win against Philadelphia we could do it.

14

IN YOUR HONOR

IF THE TRIUMPHANT home opener against Atlanta was the most historic game ever played by a Saints team, surely the game against Philadelphia was the most critical. A win would propel the team and its fans one step closer to their ultimate dream: a black-and-gold Super Bowl.

By defeating the New York Giants in their first-round play-off game, the Eagles had earned a return visit to the Big Easy, where things had not been so easy for them back in October. The winner of this game would advance to the NFC Championship. The Eagles had been to that game before. In fact, they had made a few Super Bowl appearances. But for the Saints—winners of just one play-off game in all their forty years of wandering the NFL desert—this was new territory.

For the two weeks leading up to the game, New Orleans exploded in an early Mardi Gras. Local talk shows, normally consumed with news about Katrina recovery efforts—or the lack thereof—devoted hours and hours to Saints talk. It wasn't hard to do. Nobody wanted to talk about anything else.

Unlike many other sports-crazed towns on the verge of a major play-off game, New Orleans had a unique perspective. This was not merely a game that would lead to another game and, ultimately, the Super Bowl. This game was a symbol of something bigger, for both the team and the city.

Months ago, New Orleans had rallied around a football team. Wisely or not, many invested all that they had left, their hopes and dreams, in the New Orleans Saints. In return, the players, coaches, the owner, and the everyday staff had invested back into the community. They clothed and fed thousands. They built homes for those who had lost theirs. They gave books and supplies to schools desperately in need, so that young people could learn. They restored playgrounds so children could forget their troubles and have fun, as children should. They had visited the sick and the elderly. The New Orleans Saints, as individuals and as an organization, had been the Good Samaritans the people needed. Yes, there was much more to be done, but for that 2006 season, they had given the people of New Orleans hope.

Part of that hope was that the Saints would beat the Eagles, and that the Seahawks would defeat Chicago, bringing the NFC Championship game to the Superdome. But fans and players alike knew that this might be the last time they were all together that season. And so, like old and dear friends, they did all that they could to make that time together special.

Pam Randazza, *owner, Black & Gold Sports Shop*

By now we were selling caps that had 2006 NFC South Champions on them, the official hat. Well, we couldn't keep enough of those in stock. They just flew out the door. We had all kinds of hats for the Saints, but that one really sold a lot. You wear that hat, and you feel like part of it, like you're part of the team. And I think they were. I think the fans were a big part of that success.

Scott Fujita, *linebacker, New Orleans Saints*

The partnership between this community and the team was something that I had never seen or felt. They felt like they were there with us. And they really, truly were. That's not just lip service.

Reggie Bush, *running back, New Orleans Saints*

I would say that every fan—everybody in the city, and everywhere we went—they made us feel special. At dinner, lunch, all over I'd see random people, and they were looking at us like we were the saviors of the city. But I never looked at it that way. We just did what we could do, what we were supposed to do. In fact, the way that they responded really inspired us. It made me want to do better.

Steve Gleason, *safety, New Orleans Saints*

I've lived in New Orleans for a few years, so I know what the team meant to the city, especially now. But getting ready for that Eagles play-off game was something completely new for me, and for everybody. The fans we'd see weren't just saying, "Beat the Eagles" and things like that. They were coming up to all of us and just making sure we knew how much all of this meant to them.

Drew Brees, *quarterback, New Orleans Saints*

What impressed me was I had more people come up to me, on a daily basis, and say "Thank you. Thank you for coming to our city and helping us rebuild." It was all about New Orleans. It wasn't so much about, "Hey, nice game. Nice win." That sort of thing. They just wanted us to know that, win or lose, they appreciated what we had meant to them. At times, that was a little hard to handle.

Abbe Garfinkel, *fan*

We were still living in the trailer, but it just didn't seem as bad. We had put Saints stuff all around "the den," and I had Sean Payton covering my refrigerator. We bought those flags to go on the cars. I wanted so badly to be at that game against the Eagles but there really was just no way. There weren't any tickets, so we were going to have a party in the trailer—own little skybox, our luxury suite.

Kenny Wilkerson, *sideline reporter, WWW Radio*

There may have been other things going on in sports, or even in the world, but on our station all anybody wanted to talk about was the Saints. I guess they were just so tired of talking about Katrina and insurance and all of that bad stuff. This was good stuff, and they just couldn't get enough of it.

Billy Cundiff, *placekicker, New Orleans Saints*

Before the Philly game, they declared a day Black-and-Gold Day in the city, and everybody was wearing black and gold. I mean, everybody. That just wouldn't work anywhere else. All of the schoolkids were wearing black and gold. I went into Walgreens to get a few things, and every single person there was wearing black and gold— that is, except me. Here I was, a Saints football player, and I was the only person in the whole store not wearing black and gold.

Bobby Hebert, *former quarterback, New Orleans Saints*

Leading up to that game, it was just like leading up to the Falcons. There wasn't really any trash-talking the Eagles or anything like that. It was mostly just about how good the team was and how much they liked Sean Payton and Drew Brees and all of the players. You really couldn't find callers to say something bad, even just to make it more interesting. You know, add some controversy.

Mickey Loomis, *general manager, New Orleans Saints*

That time between the Carolina game and the Eagles game in the play-offs was just magical. This whole season had been really special, but that time was unique. We certainly hoped that we would be hosting the NFC Championship game if we won, which would have been nice, but we had to also try to stay focused on this game. First, we had to practice not knowing which team to prepare for, but then once we knew it would be the Eagles, we had to just focus on that. I think Coach Payton did a wonderful job of keeping the team focused.

On January 6, 2007, the Associated Press named Saints head coach Sean Payton NFL Coach of the Year, the most prestigious honor among professional coaches.

Drew Brees

We have a truly great coach in Sean Payton. We all believe in him. He suits us very well.

Joe Horn, *wide receiver, New Orleans Saints*

Payton was tough. He was a new head coach, and he wanted to put his foot on the ground and establish that this was a new beginning. In our profession, football, you don't start a new beginning by coming in and making it easy. It has to be hard. It worked out well. We won football games.

Abbe Garfinkel

It went from "He's going to crash and burn like all of the rest" to "Coach of the Year." I was wrong. Sean, I was wrong. Okay?

Sean Payton, *head coach, New Orleans Saints*

The award goes to a head coach who has a great coaching staff, guys who spend a lot of time and late nights at the office coming up with the right plans to make our guys successful. It was a reflection on so many people, not just on me.

When I first interviewed with Mickey Loomis, we talked about goals and things we needed to do to move in the right direction. He was extremely supportive and on board with identifying what we wanted from a Saints player or employee. There's an awful lot of time spent by our scouts, Mickey and his staff, our players, Tom Benson and Rita Benson-LeBlanc. I was excited on behalf of those people, and I mean that.

It was great, and I will always be grateful, but I really had to get us ready for Philadelphia. We had played them before, but this was nine weeks later. They had some guys on offense that were not playing before. They had Jeff Garcia at quarterback now, in place of Donovan McNabb. They are two very different players, but certainly Philadelphia had responded to the way Jeff played. They were on a roll.

You were looking at two teams that had won their divisions. They won the NFC East and we won the NFC South. I knew it was going to be exciting, and that the Superdome would be a great environment.

Quint Davis, *founder and producer, New Orleans Jazz & Heritage Festival*

Without a doubt, we were going to have a big party before the play-off game. I mean, that goes without saying. We brought back our good friends the Rebirth Brass Band and New Orleans blues legend Luther Kent. The Steve Miller Band was there, too.

Rita Benson-LeBlanc, *owner/executive vice president, New Orleans Saints*

We asked our fans to come early for the food, the music, and festivities and then to cheer as loudly as they could against the Eagles. Our fans were our secret weapon.

Quint Davis

The event was not just a concert or party, it was a pep rally of sorts to warm up the fans for the game. We wanted every fan in the Superdome to be really excited and ready for kickoff.

Kenny Wilkerson

It was crazy outside of the dome. Before the Atlanta game, it was really all about just being there and being happy that the Superdome was open and that the team was back. This was something else entirely. I mean, it was really out of control. It was just insane.

Doug Thornton, *general manager, Superdome*

Like before, we had people showing up the day before the game. They just wanted to be here. In fact, by the time the game got here, there were a lot more people down here than we could have fit in the dome. I knew that a lot of them didn't have tickets. They just wanted to be part of it, part of the excitement, to share this moment, this experience.

Anthony Canatella, *deputy superintendent, New Orleans Police Department*

Oh, definitely. There were more people there who didn't have tickets than people who did, probably two, maybe three times as many. Look, people here, we grow up with Mardi Gras, where you just get your beer or whatever and find yourself a spot and have a good time. Next thing you know, you're dancing with some people you never met before. That's how we are down here. If they think it's going to be a good place to party, they show up. So, they showed up and had a party.

Quint Davis

It looked like there were a million people around the Superdome. It was just so fun and exciting. It was like Mardi Gras down there.

Bobby Hebert

It was bigger than Mardi Gras.

Sammy Marten, *fan*

There I am with no ticket, but I went down to the Superdome anyway. It was awesome. The funniest thing I saw was Saint Elvis. Like I said, I live in Memphis and we see those Elvis guys all the time and they all look the same, kind of. You know, white jumpsuit and big old sideburns, saying "Thank you very much." So here's this guy in a gold jumpsuit with a big fleur-de-lis on his back saying stuff like, "Who dat? Thank you very much." I laughed my ass off.

Kenny Wilkerson

Inside the dome was really loud again. I mean, really loud. This was it, you know, the big time.

With a capacity crowd inside the Superdome, huge crowds outside, and millions more watching on television, the pomp and pageantry of the NFL play-offs began. But, as is always the case in New Orleans, there was a little lagniappe. The fans who had overcome so much were rewarded by the Saints.

All eyes turned to the Superdome's enormous video screens as *In Your Honor*, a video tribute to the fans, began to play. Unlike most other game-time reels, which show team highlights, this showed highlights of the fans in the seats. Accompanied by the Foo Fighters' song "In Your Honor," the film showed everyone's joy and unconquerable determination. With their enthusiasm and their energy, New Orleanians had transcended the role of fan just as their team had transcended the game of football.

As the video came to a close, and the crowd roared its approval, yet another surprise appeared. As in most stadiums, the walls of the Superdome have banners honoring Saints greats such as Archie Manning and Ricky Jackson; Jim Finks, the GM who brought the Saints to respectability; and Dave Dixon, who brought the dome to life. The walls also boast two shiny gold banners commemorating the team's two previous division crowns. When a gold banner began to unfurl, the crowd roared even louder for what was sure to be their third division banner. It was not.

This banner did not honor the team on the field; it honored the team in the stands. It honored the fans, the season-ticket holders who had shown incredible faith in the Saints and, against all odds and conventional wisdom, sold out the Superdome for the very first time. The banner, of course, represented all of the fans that had made 2006 a year to remember, no matter where they were.

What was already the most historic game in franchise history soon became one of the most thrilling, too. By game's end, the team exorcised the last of the demons that had haunted them for so long.

After trading punts with the Eagles, Deuce McAllister rumbled from midfield to the Eagles' 22, and the Saints got the first score of the game, a field goal off the foot of John Carney.

The defense, playing perhaps their finest game of the entire season, stuffed Philly's Cornell Bukholter and harassed quarterback Jeff Garcia out of the pocket. They would maintain pressure throughout the game.

A dazzling Reggie Bush reception for 25 yards and a 35-yard completion to Devery Henderson had the Saints rattling the Eagles' cage at their own 4-yard line. But the Eagles' vaunted defense dropped Deuce for a 1-yard loss as the first quarter came to a close. The Saints, far ahead on the stats, had only 3 points on the scoreboard. Unable to penetrate the end zone on this drive, they settled for 3 more points from Carney.

For Philadelphia, Jeff Garcia, the cagey veteran playing in place of Donovan McNabb, threw a perfect 75-yard touchdown pass. On the other end of the pass was Donte Stallworth, the receiver the Saints had traded away earlier in the year. Would that trade come back to haunt the Saints as similar deals had in the past?

No, it wouldn't. These Saints had beaten worse adversity before. At the end of an impressive 78-yard drive that would include 3 clutch third-down conversions, Reggie Bush used his dazzling footwork to shift direction, and, cutting from left to right, covered the 4 yards needed. He found room just inside the end zone pylon to give the Saints a 13–7 advantage.

The offensive fireworks continued. Philadelphia mounted an equally impressive drive that also included a number of third-down conversions. The Eagles took a 1-point lead when Brain Westbrook dove in for a touchdown from 1 yard out. And the next drive, Drew Brees's Hail Mary pass to Marques Colston, was ruled an incompletion as the first half ended.

The opening kick of the second half looked as if it would prove Saints fans' darkest fears true. Brian Westbrook raced 62 yards through Saints coverage for a touchdown to put the Eagles up 21–13. But, as they had done all season, the

Saints answered the challenge. Two key receptions by Billy Miller set up a heroic, hard-fought 5-yard touchdown run by Deuce McAllister that will go down in Saints history.

With the entire Eagles defense on his back, McAllister trudged across the line of scrimmage, his teammates pushing and pulling him toward a touchdown. It was as if the entire team—every player and every coach and every fan and every living thing in the Superdome, and all the saints above—had willed him into that end zone. Chants of "Deuce! Deuce! Deuce!" filled the Superdome and reverberated from the rafters.

When the referee's whistle blew and the touchdown was signaled, Deuce McAllister was lying in the lush green of the Superdome turf. His helmet was gone, lost somewhere along the way, and the white jerseys of Eagle defenders were piled on top of him. The drive symbolized what the journey of the 2006 season had all been about. With a strength that can only be found from within, Deuce relentlessly pushed on. With his own will, and with the help of others, he had reached the goal. Just a year before, Deuce had been a broken player, his future as uncertain as the place he came from. Both he and the entire Gulf Coast had overcome so much. It was only fitting that he made that play.

After an all-too-familiar Superdome sight—a muffed pitch from Drew Brees to Reggie Bush—the Saints made an impressive stand on defense. And then Deuce McAllister would score yet another touchdown to hold off the Eagles and take the 2006 Saints to the NFC Championship game.

Mickey Loomis

Deuce carrying five guys, and our whole team pushing and fighting and scratching into the end zone, that's the play that I think sums up the season for me. There are all of these metaphors and things in sports that symbolize your team and your region. I think that is ours. I mean, biting, fighting, scratching, doing whatever we can, just staying on our feet and grinding away, finding a way to get to the end zone.

And it just couldn't have been more fitting that it was Deuce McAllister that carried us in that game. Remember, he's from Mississippi, and he had to deal with the hurricane there as well. Then he tears his ACL and is out and has to go through a long rehab. He was uncertain about his career. So, just like New Orleans, here is this guy, fighting and rebuilding his career, and he carries us in the biggest play at the biggest moment in Saints history.

Sean Payton

That was an exciting win for this team, this organization and this city. I couldn't be more proud of this group of guys that fought and battled and did whatever it took to win.

Deuce getting that touchdown, with all those guys on his back and he just keeps going and going—that was incredible. That was amazing, unforgettable.

Scott Fujita

That was just one of those moments in time that you never want to forget. Deuce has put together a lot of those. I remember watching that from the sideline, and it was on the front page of the newspaper the next day. I think I remember Jeff Faine probably more than anyone else as part of that pile, pushing Deuce into the end zone. Somebody took a picture just a second later. It was in the paper, too: Jeff Faine standing in the end zone with his arms up. I'll never forget that.

Steve Gleason

If you need one guy from your team in a situation like that, with all that pressure and everything else, you want a guy like Deuce. That was his moment. It was his destiny to be our guy at that moment.

Deuce McAllister, *running back, New Orleans Saints*

I had a lot of help from the offensive line and my fullback, Mike Karney, on that run. I am a big guy at 230 pounds, and he's 255, and he was pushing me. You have to be determined on a play like that and make sure that the ball doesn't get stripped.

Kenny Wilkerson

When Drew went down to take a knee and let time run, the whole place just erupted. It went crazy. People were jumping up and down and dancing. You just couldn't help but get caught up in the emotion.

Bobby Hebert

I was cheering in the press box and waving my rally rag and whatever. They said, "Oh Bobby, you can't do that. They might throw you out." Let them. Throw me out. I wanted to be out there with the fans anyway. I wanted to be part of this, all this fun and excitement.

Doug Thornton

The fans stayed right where they were. Nobody, not a soul, headed toward the exits. They just kept cheering.

Steve Gleason

Oh man, what a feeling. I just can't tell you. It was the best feeling I have ever had. We had done it. They had done it. Everybody had done it. We all stayed out there and were shaking hands, high-fiving and trying to share this with the fans. And they were all still there, right where they had been all night—all year, really.

Scott Fujita

People did not want to leave. I was lucky. My wife was sitting up in the stands with my family. Well, the team eventually went into the locker room, but she stayed out there for another fifteen or twenty minutes, and she had a digital camera. It's not even a video recorder, just one of those cameras that record like thirty-second intervals. It was so loud and so exciting that she thought she'd take a video of the crowd and how many people stuck around after the game. The picture is real gritty, but she recorded for like thirty seconds, panning around the whole Superdome. This was long after the game and the fans are all still there.

Actually at the end of the video, my wife turns and gets a quick clip of Steve Gleason's girlfriend, Michelle. Michelle is a real New Orleans native, and her family lives and dies with the Saints. It's a shot of Michelle jumping up and down with tears streaming down her face. I keep that clip on my computer back home in California so that any time I need goose bumps, I can just look at it.

Anthony Canatella

After that game, nobody was leaving. They were all just staying right where they were. After a while, security had to go tell some people it was time to go, some a little more firmly than others. They weren't causing any trouble; they just wanted it to last a little longer.

Somebody asked me, "Do you think there is going to be rioting or any of that foolishness that goes on in other cities after big games?"

I told him, "People here, they just want to have a good time. They want to make love, not trouble."

Sammy Marten

I had watched the game with some people in a bar down in the warehouse district. As soon as it was over, people started pouring out into the streets. There are a lot of bars and music places down there. Pretty soon, the streets were packed. Everybody was happy. I didn't see any trouble, just happy people. This was the happiest I had seen this town in a long time.

15

IF I'M DREAMING, DON'T WAKE ME

THE 2006 SEASON had been like a dream for the Saints and their fans, and in beating the Philadelphia Eagles, they made sure the dream would last at least one more week. The problem with dreams is that sooner or later you have to wake up.

In the NFL, one thing is certain, the Super Bowl has a date, a time, and a place picked out and set years in advance. Super Bowl XLI was set for February 4, 2007, at Dolphin Stadium in sunny Miami Beach—and the Saints were just one game away from playing there. That one game, however, was against the Bears at Soldier Field in the cold, inhospitable Chicago. The Monsters of the Midway owned the home-field advantage in the play-offs, having finished their regular season atop the NFC North with a 13–3 record, and by beating the Seattle Seahawks 27–24 in the previous round.

One question that begged to be asked was, "How would the Saints respond after another emotional game?" In week three, they had beaten the Falcons while reopening the Superdome. They followed that triumph with a loss at Carolina in week five. Weeks fourteen and fifteen had literally been a game of cowboys and Indians. The Saints corralled the Cowboys at Dallas, but were scalped by the Redskins soon after. After the ecstasy of their play-off win over the Eagles, would they be able to marshal their mental and physical reserves, or would they be blown away in the Windy City?

Drew Brees, *quarterback, New Orleans Saints*

I had only played in one other play-off game. That was in San Diego, and it was a loss. So I was like many guys on our team: I had never won a play-off game. A lot of guys on the team hadn't ever even *played* in a postseason game, not until that year, so I think we were all searching for that win. You certainly don't want to go through a season like we had and then lose in the first round of the play-offs. That win against the Eagles was just really a great way to cap off what had been a very special season for everyone in New Orleans. We wanted that feeling to continue.

Sean Payton, *head coach, New Orleans Saints*

I don't think that being excited after a win really affects how you perform a week later. We had played some very good football teams, every week. No matter whether you win a game or lose a game, you move on and you prepare for the next one. You look at the tape and change or adjust what you need to, but you really prepare the same.

Scott Fujita, *linebacker, New Orleans Saints*

We all knew that this was going to be a good team we were playing. They had finished their season 13–3, and they were really well coached. Lovie Smith is great, and so nobody was taking it lightly.

Reggie Bush, *running back, New Orleans Saints*

I really wasn't thinking about the Super Bowl, to be honest. This was my first year in the league, and we were playing for the NFC Championship. That was the game that week. That's how I looked at it. We had won the NFC South, now let's win the whole NFC and then see what happens if that falls into place.

Steve Gleason, *safety, New Orleans Saints*

Like I said before, if you can imagine it, then it can happen. Nothing is impossible. A year ago this franchise finished 3–13. We were living out of suitcases and hotel rooms. We didn't know where we going to play, or if we were even coming back to New Orleans. We really didn't know if there would be enough fans to keep the team there, and nobody really thought that we were going to do anything much this season. And here we were, with the greatest fans in the world buying up all the tickets and setting records—and we're playing for the NFC Championship. I was just like, okay, bring it on.

Kenny Wilkerson, *sideline reporter, WWL Radio*

If anything, Sean Payton keeps this team pretty even-keeled. At practice and all during the week, they were getting ready just like you'd expect them to. They didn't act like they were overconfident, but they certainly didn't act like they were intimidated by the Bears, either.

Sammy Marten, *fan*

I guess maybe it seems like I have family everywhere, but my cousin Frank lives in Chicago, and he knew somebody who could get tickets for my brothers and me. I would have probably driven to Chicago anyway, but this time I actually had a ticket. My little truck is a Toyota Tacoma, and it's black. I spent an hour putting fleur-de-lis stickers all over it. It was like my own personal Saintsmobile. I drove it right into downtown Chicago like that. I was wearing my Saints jersey and playing my Saints CD as loud as I could with the windows down. It was freezing cold, and I had the windows down in my truck shouting "Who dat?" at everybody. They probably thought I was crazy. I don't know, maybe I was.

Leonard Rolfes, *fan*

I grew up in Lafayette and went to school in New Orleans, so I had always been a Saints fan. I couldn't go to Miami, so Chicago was going to be it for me. I just couldn't believe what was happening. Forty years of futility, and now they are one game away from the Super Bowl. I booked the plane ticket and the room before I knew if I could get tickets. I was going with two childhood friends from Lafayette.

Abbe Garfinkel, *fan*

I thought maybe we could go to Chicago. You know, maybe since it was going to be so cold not that many people would be going. Maybe we could splurge and get tickets. Boy was I wrong.

Kenny Wilkerson

The visiting team in a big game like that really doesn't get all that many tickets, so there were a lot more people trying to go than there were seats. In fact, you really couldn't get plane tickets, either. Chicago is a busy city without a game like this, and there were not enough seats available. So people were taking the train, driving, hitchhiking, whatever it took. And that's if they had a ticket.

Leonard Rolfes

I still needed tickets, and I wasn't going to buy any outside of the stadium like I used to in the old days, because now they might be selling counterfeit ones. I needed three seats, and Ticketmaster was out or not selling to people outside of Chicago. I'm not sure what the deal was, but that was no good. I got into a bidding war on StubHub, but ultimately lost there. I was watching eBay like a hawk.

Bobby Hebert, *former quarterback, New Orleans Saints*

The Bears fans certainly wanted to go, and that's a big city, so they were taking all they could get, too. And Soldier Field doesn't hold 75,000 or whatever it did when it was built. It's the same size as most in the league, like 66,000 or something like that. So people who had tickets could sell them for really whatever they wanted. We heard about people paying thousands of dollars for tickets.

Sammy Marten

Some idiot in Chicago asked me if I wanted to sell my ticket. Here I am in Chicago in a Saints jersey shouting "Who Dat?" at strangers, and he thinks I want to sell my ticket. I said, "Do I look that stupid?"

Leonard Rolfes

Section 318, Row 2. We paid $467 per ticket.

Michelle Babineaux, *owner, Michaul's Cajun Dance Hall*

I kept asking people where they were going to watch the game, and there just weren't places doing a big thing for the fans. So I said, "We have to do something."

I have this big place, and we weren't open as a restaurant anymore. We were just doing a few private functions. So I thought, well, I'll do something for the fans here.

I just wanted it to be somewhere fun for the locals to go and be able to watch this game in a big group with lots of other fans. You know, if you couldn't be in Chicago at the game, this would be almost as good. We had 800 spaces and they were all gone in less than forty-eight hours. I wasn't trying to make money, not that I didn't need it, but I thought it would be good, and it was. It was a blast.

We had Cajun-fried turkey, jambalaya, red beans and rice, catfish bites, bread pudding and rum sauce, and then some more stuff we whipped up. It was also during Carnival season in New Orleans, so we had King Cake, lots of King Cake. That was donated by Haydel's Bakery. The owner, David, is a sweetheart; he donated it for the fans.

WWL did the pregame show from here with Bobby Hebert, so it was really Cajun. A bunch of former Saints showed up, too.

Bobby Hebert

That was great down at Michaul's with the Cajun food and all of the fans watching on big screens all through the place. Maybe we weren't in Chicago, but we didn't have to eat a stadium hot dog or that sausage they sell there, either. We were eating good.

Abbe Garfinkel

We cooked some food and put on the jerseys and got ready to watch the game in our FEMA skybox on wheels.

Daniel Garroway, *fan*

The Saturday before the Saints played Chicago, my brother had made a Saints music CD with about fifteen songs, and we piled into the back of my dad's old truck with a boom box. My sisters, who were selling Girl Scout cookies, joined us, and we drove through several neighborhoods in Mandeville with the Saints songs blaring so everyone could hear.

It seemed to make everyone we met very happy and fired up for the Saints, and my sisters sold a lot of cookies. I told them that they were lucky that the Saints were doing so well, which probably helped them sell more boxes of cookies. My sister Sydney met her sales goal, and as a result will be going to Georgia this summer for a Girl Scout trip.

Scott Fujita

At the hotel that morning, real early, I had heard all of this noise, and I thought, what the heck is all of that? It turns out it was thousands of our fans. They were here in Chicago. That made me really feel great.

Steve Gleason

In the hotel the night before the game, they had a big celebration going on. I mean, part of me wanted to go down there, maybe even just for a minute, but you can't think about that. I knew I had to be rested and mentally ready for this game. I was glad they were here, but I had to be ready.

Sammy Marten

We got to the team hotel for a pep rally before the game. At those things, if you're there then you're all friends. I don't know how many people there were, but it seemed like 5,000. Everybody had Saints jerseys and Saints stuff on, and then we Who Datted all the way over to the stadium. I have no idea how far it was, but I think it was over a mile.

The Bears fans had been nasty from day one, and now they were shouting at us. I do recall a few snowballs being thrown while we were marching, but 5,000 crazy Who Dats was a little intimidating for their little pockets of fans along the way. Soldier Field, now that was a different story entirely.

Leonard Rolfes

They did not do anything to make us feel welcome, that's for sure. The Bears fans did not want us there at all.

Kenny Wilkerson

It was what's considered "a hostile environment," which means it's not nice. And this was before the game. Of course, it got worse as the game went on.

Sammy Marten

When we got to the stadium, that's when the BS really intensified, and, of course, we all had to split up, so we were really outnumbered in there. When I got up to the ticket guy, he had to read my sign to make sure it didn't say anything offensive, so I showed it to him. It said "AIN'TS NO MORE." He said, "Ain'ts no more what?" I just stared at him for a minute, then walked in.

Scott Fujita

Even in warm-ups you could see that their fans were really getting into it. It was kind of rowdy. I could see some of our guys, because they were the only people not wearing blue, but they were kind of spread out.

Sammy Marten

My dad had been a lifelong Saints fan, but he died in 1993. The year before he died, I had given him one of those full-length Saints team coats. He really loved it, but didn't get the chance to wear it much. So I got it back from my mother, and that's what I wore at the game. I had Dad's picture with me right there in the pocket, too. He would have wanted to be there, so for my brothers and me it was like he was.

When we got to our seats, there was this fat, obnoxious guy there who kept telling us that we could not sit there and cheer for the Saints. He said he'd done three tours of Vietnam—which is great and all, and I respect him, but what does that have to do with the game? He kept telling us that the spirits of Walter Payton and Brain Piccolo were watching over the Bears. Every time the Saints did something good, he would start praying to Walter Payton and Brian Piccolo. "Oh Walter, oh Sweetness, please help us now." I guess maybe it worked.

I had my sign, and every time I held it up, I got bombarded with snowballs, cups—anything they could throw. There wasn't that much snow, really, so they were throwing like snow golf balls. I got a few in the face. I'd like to say it was all just good, clean fun, but it wasn't. This was like warfare.

Legendary New Orleans sportscaster Buddy Diliberto had once been banned from the Saints' team plane during the ownership of John Mecom. Although Buddy loved the Saints dearly, he was often the most vocal of the team's critics in the local media. Asked once if the Saints would ever go to the Super Bowl, he responded that it would be a cold day in hell before that would happen.

Soldier Field in January may not be hell, but it wasn't exactly heaven, either. And it was cold. A light snow fell throughout the game.

The Saints showed flashes of brilliance that—against a lesser team—might have taken them to Miami. But, in the end, the thing that had most worried Coach Sean Payton back in the preseason came back to haunt them. The Saints turned the ball over 4 times, 1 fumble each from Marques Colston and Michael Lewis in the first quarter, and an interception and fumble by Drew Brees in the last.

In the first half, the Bears put 13 unanswered points on the scoreboard. Coming slow out of the gate, Drew Brees and Marques Colston connected for a 13-yard touchdown to bring the Saints to within 6 as they went to halftime.

The second half opened with the longest play in NFC Championship game history as running back Reggie Bush silenced the hometown fans with an 88-yard touchdown reception that brought the Saints to within 2 points.

Uncharacteristically, the rookie sensation broke into what can best be described as the Bush Boogie. The Bears' future hall-of-fame linebacker Brian Urlacher, just a few yards away, did not join in. But that would be the last time that day that any Saint had any reason to dance. For the Who Dat Nation, the party was over.

With a chance to take a 1-point advantage, kicker Billy Cundiff was sent out to attempt a 47-yard field goal. In the controlled climate of the Superdome, the kick most likely would have been money in the bank. In the cold and wet of Chicago, however, it fell short. It was the last serious threat the Saints made at the Bears' heavily defended end zone.

Then a penalty was called on Drew Brees for intentional grounding in the end zone, giving the Bears their only points of the third period. Heading into what would prove to be the final quarter of the 2006 season for the Saints and their faithful, the Bears held a slight 4-point lead. But by the end of that quarter it was a blowout. A 33-yard touchdown pass from Rex Grossman to Bernard Berrian, followed by touchdown runs of by Cedric Benson and Thomas Jones put the final score at Bears 39, Saints 14.

Billy Cundiff, *placekicker, New Orleans Saints*

It was 47 yards in the freezing cold, and the ground was wet, so it wasn't an easy kick, but that's what I am paid to do. With a kick like that, especially in weather like they had in Chicago that night, you really have to hit it just perfectly. If it had been in the Superdome, no problem. But I guess I just didn't hit it exactly like I needed to. It just wasn't quite long enough. Trust me on this: kickers take missing really hard. Nobody, and I mean nobody, felt worse about that than I did.

Sammy Marten

Once Cundiff missed the kick, you could feel that it was over. It was just a matter of time, and the Bears fans started really getting loud. They were shouting "We Dat" at us. "Who Dat? Da Bears, Dat Who." And that sort of thing. I guess it was funny for them. I mean, they were winning and all. But I really hate them. To this day, I hate them. Who do I hate? Bears fans.

Kenny Wilkerson

You hate to see it end like that, but it had really been a great season and a great story. This wasn't Hollywood. It was real life.

Sean Payton

It's tough when you play in the postseason. The finality of a loss stings. There isn't a next week again until next year. The way the league is now, you know that some of your guys won't be back with you next year, so it's the end of *this* team. And this team in particular was probably the best team I have been around as far as togetherness and putting the team first. I think that made this loss hurt that much more.

John Stinchcomb, *tackle, New Orleans Saints*

If you're playing in a championship game, you can't play the way we did. We did not play well. I did not play well.

Drew Brees

Anytime you get that close to the Super Bowl you've accomplished something. Sure, it didn't feel good right then. You don't want to end your season like that, with a loss. But if you go to the play-offs, you end your season with a loss unless you win the Super Bowl. Of all those teams, only the Colts got to end with a win. And from where we started a year ago, I think we had a lot to be proud of.

Michelle Babineaux

I'll say this: not one fan left before the game was over. Nobody said anything bad. They might have been upset when something didn't go right, but nobody said anything bad about that team. These people knew that the team was doing their best.

Leonard Rolfes

Oh well. For my whole life we'd been asking, "Is it next year yet?" But this year, division champs and one game away from the Super Bowl? I'll take it.

Sammy Marten

After the game we just sort of soaked it all in, and you can't help but feel down. But, really, it had been great. We were going to my cousin's for dinner. He had some friends there, and there was also a Catholic priest, so the cursing was kept to a minimum. My cousin is a Bears fan, and he took a few shots at us, but then everybody really started saying how great it had all been. His friends were all Bears fans, too, and they said what I think everybody thought: If it wasn't going to be the Bears, they hoped it would have been the Saints. If the Saints had been playing anybody else, they would have been pulling for us. Honestly, though, I am so glad that the Colts beat the Bears in the Super Bowl. So glad.

COMING HOME

WHEN THE CLOCK at Soldier Field ticked down to its final seconds, New Orleans' dreams of Super Bowl glory had vanished. With the realization that their Cinderella season was over, the Saints removed their glass-slipper cleats. The ball was over. It was time to go home.

For the team, 2006 had been a hard-fought battle that tested their patience, their faith and their determination. With months of hard work, and just a tiny bit of luck, they'd compiled a winning record, and a record-setting play-off performance for the franchise. But this year, unlike most seasons in professional sports, the Saints' success could not be measured in scores or statistics.

In their final hours as a team, the Saints' journey would continue just as it had begun—returning to the city of New Orleans. But this time they were going back to a very different place. What was once battered and beaten now stood strong and proud. Back in September, the team's arrival had brought smiles where there had been sadness. With their actions and their character, they had motivated and given hope to an entire region, just when the people there needed it most.

And once again, for this trip home, something extra and unexpected—a little lagniappe—was thrown in at just the right time. It had been a battle to get to Chicago, and it would be an ordeal to get home as well. Now it was the players who were battered and beaten and carrying the sorrow of dreams unrealized. Just as the Saints had carried the people through their terrible, difficult times, the fans now turned out to carry the Saints. For forty years, through good times and bad, New Orleans had always stuck by its team. Tonight would be no exception. They came together and rallied around these all-too-human beings, their beloved Saints, just when they needed it most.

Bobby Hebert, *former quarterback, New Orleans Saints*

All the callers were calling in, saying how great the season had been. There are usually complaints. They usually say, "Well, if they had done this one thing differently, or that one thing differently, maybe they would have won." But it was all positive. I think the fans knew that these guys, they played as hard as they could.

Billy Cundiff, *placekicker, New Orleans Saints*

In my mind, I just keep thinking back over the kick. Maybe if I had hit it this way or that way, it might have gone a few extra yards. It just kept going through my mind.

Kenny Wilkerson, *sideline reporter, WWL Radio*

I don't want to say that the team was down, but they weren't happy. Let me put it this way: you could see that they all just wanted to get home.

Abbe Garfinkel, *fan*

So, we turned off the TV and started cleaning up our little FEMA skybox. I walked outside to get some fresh air, and I looked at my old house. It was a lot better than it had been when the season started. I thought back on how bad it was and how really depressed I had been. Then I walked past my cars with their Saints flags, and it put a smile on my face.

Scott Fujita, *linebacker, New Orleans Saints*

I wish we had won, but I think the guys all understood how much we had accomplished for the team and ourselves and for the fans. When you lose a game like that, you want to move on as quickly as you can, because your routine is over now. During the season you have the next game to get ready for, to take you mind off of losing, but this was the last game of the year, so we were going to have a long time to think about it. I just wanted to get home and see my wife and relax.

Reggie Bush, *running back, New Orleans Saints*

We had a great run, and we gave it our best shot. We did more than I think anybody could have predicted. Nobody could have predicted us in the NFC Championship game, but still I wish we had won. We were not satisfied. It was time to go home, rest a little and then move on and start getting ready for next year.

Billy Cundiff

The team charter plane had been parked in the wrong place or something, so we had to wait while they moved it. It was down a hill or something, and then there had been snow and so they had to de-ice the plane, too. They had this little truck thing that worked like a tugboat trying to move us. That one wasn't big enough, so they brought out another one of these tugboat things to tug the first little tugboat thing. So we were stuck there on the plane for a couple of hours.

Sean Payton, *head coach, New Orleans Saints*

All of the guys wanted to get home to their families and friends, but we were stuck in Chicago for what seemed like forever. That was tough, because we just really needed to get our minds on something else. It was over, and we needed to move on, but we were still in Chicago.

Bobby Hebert

You know, a lot of times people go out to the airport to greet the team, so we had callers saying that they were going and that everybody should go. So that starts taking shape, but the plane was delayed at first. It wasn't going to be real late, you know, maybe an hour. It was cold and starting to rain outside, so I was telling people to hold on and go get something to eat so they wouldn't be stuck out in the rain, waiting.

Michelle Babineaux, *owner, Michaul's Cajun Dance Hall*

I heard people as they were leaving, saying, "We need to go to the airport." It seemed like almost everybody there was going out to the airport to meet the team.

Abbe Garfinkel

I had thought about going out there to greet the team, but it was a long drive. I figured maybe we had waited too long, but I heard Bobby saying that the plane was still in Chicago, and he was giving the new arrival time. I don't think I even heard what time they would be in, but I knew I could drive there faster than the time it took to fly from Chicago. I looked at Sean Payton's pictures on my refrigerator, and then I just announced, "We're going!"

And off we went, flags fluttering all the way to the airport.

Bobby Hebert

The fans kept calling saying how they were bringing their kids and all. It just seemed like more and more people were going. So I had to keep breaking into my show with the callers to give these updates about where the plane was and when it would be in. The last time I was breaking in and giving updates like that? That was when Katrina was about to make landfall. It was nice to be giving people good news instead. I was telling the fans that it was cold and rainy, so bundle up and bring something warm to drink, like hot chocolate. I was on the air doing that until the plane almost landed.

Anthony Canatella, *deputy superintendent, New Orleans Police Department*

I would have gone, but I had work. Working at the Superdome for every game like I do, I see the players after. They always stop and say hello, shake my hand. Sometimes I get something autographed for a friend or a kid. So I really wanted to go, but I couldn't.

But my son, that's another story. He was racing down there like the whole city. He calls his girlfriend and a few friends and they head off to the airport.

Anthony Canatella Jr., *fan*

We got out there and got a really good spot right on the barricade near the gate to the airport. Then the Kenner Police told people about the plane being delayed some more. It was cold and drizzling rain, and we hadn't eaten anything since the game.

We asked the people next to us to hold our place and we all went to Denny's. A bunch of people must have had the same idea. Pretty soon the place was full of soaking wet people in Saints jerseys.

When we went back, the crowd may have looked thinner, but it had stretched way out. We walked a pretty good ways past a lot of fans to get back where we had been.

Bobby Hebert

We had people calling in on cell phones saying, "There's still time. Everybody come on out to the airport." In all my years, both as a player and in the media, I had never seen this kind of unity before.

Harry Connick Jr., *singer*

There was a time when we never thought they'd play another game there, much less be a play-off team. It was the single biggest hope-builder New Orleans had. Those players and coaches need to be shown a lot of love, because they've turned this city around.

George W. Bush, *president of the United States*

The New Orleans Saints football team represents what's happened down there. There is a resurgence, there is a renewal. That was very uplifting. The spirit of the people down there is strong.

Ken Trahan, *manager, Saints Hall of Fame*

The New Orleans Saints have played perhaps the biggest role of any entity in bringing this community back. They are a unifying force. People that are poor, people that are wealthy. People that are black, people that are white. They have differences that are beyond belief. In real life, their differences are so vast they don't even communicate. In many cases they don't like each other, or trust each other.

But when they show up at that Superdome, they're slapping each other on the back, giving each other high fives, jumping up and down—and it's all about one thing. For all of our political mistakes, our business mistakes, our disagreements about race and class, on Sunday afternoon all that goes away.

I try not to get too spiritual when it comes to sports. All these people have been saying for years, "Oh, it's a curse because they built the dome over a graveyard. They named themselves the Saints, and it's sacrilegious." Then you have Holy Moses leading us to the Promised Land, and all that stuff. I don't believe any of it. But after all the pain and suffering that everybody went through, to have the Saints have this improbable season, this *miraculous* season, you just can't help but chuckle and say that God had a hand in it.

How else do you explain the fact that they go from 3–13 to the NFC Championship game? That we had a record attendance despite losing half our population? That the Superdome went from being the site of such misery to become a place of celebration beyond belief? How else do you explain it?

Quint Davis, *founder and producer, New Orleans Jazz & Heritage Festival*

That trip home took forever. I flew home on the team plane, and you could see that they all just wanted to put an end to this chapter, get something to eat and then get some rest, but we were still on the plane.

Scott Fujita

We were finally getting pretty close to New Orleans. I don't know how late we were, but it was like hours. Then somebody said that there were people at the airport. I was like, "What? We lost. It's raining."

Then I thought, well, there'll be a few people there at least. That's nice.

Reggie Bush

I thought maybe if we had won, there might be some fans, but I really didn't expect too many. But guys were saying that a bunch had showed up.

Billy Cundiff

I think some of the guys had spoken with family members in New Orleans, and they kept saying that it was a big crowd. In Dallas, when I played there, you might have a few people but never too, too many.

Anthony Canatella Jr.

We all kept waiting. Every plane that landed at the airport, people would watch to see if it turned to go off to the main terminal or not. The charter comes to a different part of the airport. Every plane, we waited and watched.

Then finally this plane lands and one of the people near me said that was the one. He had seen their plane before. It did, in fact, turn toward us, and everybody just went nuts.

Kenny Wilkerson

So we finally land, and, looking out of the plane windows, you could see that there were some people. Once the doors to the plane opened, the crowd just roared. Now the fans are outside of the gate a few hundred feet away, and you could hear them inside of the plane. That's how loud they were. That's how many of them there were, too.

Scott Fujita

There had always been people at the airport for us, but with the loss and a few hours' delay and then the rain, well, I just could not have expected a crowd that big. They were all lined up for miles and miles it seemed, from the exit area by the tarmac all the way out to Veterans Highway. It was just unbelievable, thousands and thousands of people. I wish I had had that video camera.

Drew Brees, *quarterback, New Orleans Saints*

We all got in our cars and then went through the exit, and there they were. We have this two-mile-long line of people just showing their appreciation. And, you know, this was after a loss. It took us hours to get through that line. We all stopped and shook hands with everybody and signed autographs all the way through. People had made signs and dressed up. It was crazy.

Steve Gleason, *safety, New Orleans Saints*

I kind of thought they would be there because that's how people are in New Orleans. They support you. But then I thought, well, maybe with it raining and all, they might not be there. I forgot for a minute what they had gone through. These are the same people who had lost their houses and their jobs in a hurricane. A little rain wouldn't bother them at all.

It was fantastic. They were thanking us, even though we lost. They were thanking us for the season and I was saying thank you right back. This was so cool and so perfect. Thank you, that was all I could think.

Sean Payton

I had never head coached a play-off team, so I had never coached one that had lost a play-off game, either. I really didn't know what to expect. We had gone to the Super Bowl when I was with the Giants. We had hardly anybody at the airport when we got back. And here were people as far as you good see. They were all just as happy as could be and thanking us. They were thanking us. It was truly uplifting. It was maybe as uplifting as anything all year. I was waving and when traffic stopped I was shaking hands and signing things. It was really special.

Abbe Garfinkel

I'm looking and I'm looking and finally somebody says, "There he is. That's Sean Payton."

So I look and, sure enough, there he is. I wave, and he waves back. And, you know what? He was smiling, lips wide open—smiling.

Mickey Loomis, *general manager, New Orleans Saints*

That crowd out there after Chicago was amazing. I had never seen anything like it, never experienced anything like it. Boy, you talk about lifting up spirits, because we were down. Those championship games are great when you reach them, but the fall off that cliff is pretty far. The fact that they came out for us was very uplifting for everybody in our organization.

Reggie Bush

I was shocked to see all those people there. It made me feel good. Nothing can take away the fact that we lost, but that made me feel really good. Looking back, you know, I was supposed to be the first pick in the draft and all. Now I was sure: I was glad I came to New Orleans. It's an awesome feeling when people let you know how much they want you and appreciate you. When we got home from Chicago with all those fans out there, even in the rain, well, I appreciated them too. I am glad I came to New Orleans. I'm glad that I am a Saint.

Billy Cundiff

I had missed the kick, and maybe some people think that cost the game, I don't know. But when I was driving out, I saw a friend along the barricades and he got in the car with me so we could go get something to eat. I was starving. I had my windows up, and after a minute he said, "You really need to roll the windows down and take this in."

I was a little hesitant, because I didn't want to be booed or anything. You never know what people might do. But I went ahead and rolled down the window. Nobody said a word about the kick, and they knew who I was. When we stopped once, a lady came up to the window and asked me to sign her son's jersey. I started to say that I was sorry for missing the kick, but before I could say it, she grabbed my arm through the window and squeezed it and looked right at me and said, "No! Thank you. Thank you so much. Thank you guys for everything you've done for us. We can never thank you enough."

That really got to me. I called my wife and told her what was going on. It was just truly, truly amazing. I will never forget that. I don't think it will ever happen again anywhere else. That could have only happened in New Orleans, with those fans and at that time. The whole thing was so unique in so many ways.

Mitch Landrieu, *lieutenant governor, Louisiana*

People here really hadn't had anything to brag about, and the Saints gave them that. They gave us something to feel good about and to take pride in. They gave the people some of their swagger back. People saw that good things were possible, and that things could get better. The Saints gave us hope; they gave us a reason to believe.

Scott Fujita

I have had some time to think about this. I had never been in a place where the partnership between the team and the community was so real and so genuine, like they really were in the whole thing together. It just made my experience so much more than just about football. As a player, you always hope that you are going to win a Super Bowl, and that would be great, but that's a game. This was something entirely different.

If I could wish one thing for every guy who ever plays football, it would be that just once in his career, just one time, he gets to experience something like this. I don't think anybody, fan or player, will ever forget this. We didn't bring home some big, shiny trophy, but we got this moment, what we all came together and did for each other. We didn't need a trophy. The City of New Orleans is our trophy.

APPPENDICES

NEW ORLEANS SAINTS 2006 SEASON SUMMARY

PRESEASON (1–3)

Date	Opponent	Result
08/12/06	@ Tennessee Titans	W, 19–16
08/21/06	DALLAS COWBOYS	L, 7–30
08/26/06	INDIANAPOLIS COLTS	L, 14–27
08/31/06	@ Kansas City Chiefs	L, 9–10

REGULAR SEASON (10–6)

09/10/06	@ Cleveland Browns	W, 19–14
09/17/06	@ Green Bay Packers	W, 34–27
09/25/06	ATLANTA FALCONS	W, 23–3
10/01/06	@ Carolina Panthers	L, 18–21
10/08/06	TAMPA BAY BUCCANEERS	W, 24–21
10/15/06	PHILADELPHIA EAGLES	W, 27–24
10/29/06	BALTIMORE RAVENS	L, 22–35
11/05/06	@ Tampa Bay Buccaneers	W, 31–14
11/12/06	@ Pittsburgh Steelers	L, 31–38
11/19/06	CINCINNATI BENGALS	L, 16–31
11/26/06	@ Atlanta Falcons	W, 31–13

12/03/06	SAN FRANCISCO 49ers	W, 34–10
12/10/06	@ Dallas Cowboys	W, 42–17
12/17/06	WASHINGTON REDSKINS	L, 10–16
12/24/06	@ New York Giants	W, 30–7
12/31/06	CAROLINA PANTHERS	L, 21–31

NFC DIVISIONAL PLAY-OFFS

| 01/13/06 | PHILADELPHIA EAGLES | W, 27–24 |

NFC CHAMPIONSHIP GAME

| 01/21/06 | @ Chicago Bears | L, 14–39 |

NEW ORLEANS SAINTS 2006 ROSTER

ACTIVE PLAYERS

#	NAME	POS	HT	WT	COLLEGE
20	Bellamy, Jay	S	5-11	200	Rutgers
35	Branch, Jamaal	RB	6-1	230	Colgate
9	Brees, Drew	QB	6-0	209	Purdue
70	Brown, Jammal	T	6-6	313	Oklahoma
29	Bullocks, Josh	S	6-1	207	Nebraska
25	Bush, Reggie	RB	6-0	203	Southern California
80	Campbell, Mark	TE	6-6	260	Michigan
3	Carney, John	K	5-11	185	Notre Dame
54	Clark, Danny	LB	6-2	245	Illinois
12	Colston, Marques	WR	6-4	231	Hofstra
97	Cooper, Josh	DE	6-3	265	Mississippi
18	Copper, Terrance	WR	6-0	207	East Carolina
21	Craft, Jason	CB	5-10	187	Colorado State
4	Cundiff, Billy	K	6-1	201	Drake
39	Deloatch, Curtis	CB	6-2	217	North Carolina A&T
73	Evans, Jahri	G	6-4	318	Bloomsburg
52	Faine, Jeff	C	6-3	291	Notre Dame

56	Fincher, Alfred	LB	6-1	238	Connecticut
55	Fujita, Scott	LB	6-5	250	California
37	Gleason, Steve	S	5-11	212	Washington State
76	Goodwin, Jonathan	OL	6-3	318	Michigan
94	Grant, Charles	DE	6-3	290	Georgia
28	Groce, DeJuan	CB	5-10	192	Nebraska
19	Henderson, Devery	WR	5-11	200	Louisiana State
61	Holland, Montrae	G	6-2	322	Florida State
87	Horn, Joe	WR	6-1	213	Itawamba (Miss.) CC
47	Houser, Kevin	LS	6-2	252	Ohio State
89	Jones, Jamal	WR	5-11	205	North Carolina A&T
44	Karney, Mike	FB	5-11	258	Arizona State
96	Lake, Antwan	DT	6-4	308	West Virginia
77	Leisle, Rodney	DT	6-3	315	UCLA
84	Lewis, Michael	WR	5-8	173	None
10	Martin, Jamie	QB	6-2	205	Weber State
26	McAllister, Deuce	RB	6-1	232	Mississippi
34	McKenzie, Mike	CB	6-0	194	Memphis
51	Melton, Terrence	LB	6-1	235	Rice
83	Miller, Billy	TE	6-3	252	Southern California
67	Nesbit, Jamar	G	6-4	328	South Carolina
86	Owens, John	TE	6-3	255	Notre Dame
79	Petitti, Rob	T	6-6	327	Pittsburgh
24	Scott, Bryan	S	6-1	219	Penn State
58	Shanle, Scott	LB	6-2	245	Nebraska
53	Simoneau, Mark	LB	6-0	245	Kansas State
91	Smith, Will	DE	6-3	282	Ohio State
27	Stecker, Aaron	RB	5-10	213	Western Illinois
78	Stinchcomb, Jon	T	6-5	315	Georgia
23	Stoutmire, Omar	S	5-11	205	Fresno State
64	Strief, Zach	T	6-7	349	Northwestern
22	Thomas, Fred	CB	5-9	185	Tennessee-Martin

99	Thomas, Hollis	DT	6-0	306	Northern Illinois
7	Weatherford, Steve	P	6-3	215	Illinois
98	Whitehead, Willie	DE	6-3	300	Auburn
66	Young, Brian	DT	6-2	298	Texas–El Paso

RESERVE/INJURED

50	Allen, James	LB	6-2	245	Oregon State
17	Berger, Mitch	P	6-4	228	Colorado
85	Conwell, Ernie	TE	6-2	255	Washington
41	Harper, Roman	S	6-1	200	Alabama
74	Hoffman, Augie	G	6-2	315	Boston College
33	Joseph, Keith	RB	6-2	249	Texas A&M
30	McAfee, Fred	RB	5-10	197	Mississippi College
93	Ninkovich, Rob	DE	6-2	252	Purdue
54	Polley, Tommy	LB	6-3	230	Florida State
63	Setterstrom, Chad	T	6-3	310	Northern Iowa

COACHING STAFF

Sean Payton	**Head Coach**
John Bonamego	Special Teams Coordinator
Gary Gibbs	Defensive Coordinator
Doug Marrone	Offensive Coordinator/Offensive Line
Joe Vitt	Assistant Head Coach/Linebackers
George Henshaw	Senior Offensive Assistant/Running Backs
Dennis Allen	Assistant Defensive Line
Adam Bailey	Assistant Strength and Conditioning
Pete Carmichael Jr.	Quarterbacks
Dan Dalrymple	Head Strength and Conditioning
Tom Hayes	Defensive Backs
Marion Hobby	Defensive Line

Curtis Johnson	Wide Receivers
Terry Malone	Tight Ends
Greg McMahon	Assistant Special Teams
John Morton	Offensive Assistant/Passing Game
Tony Oden	Defensive Assistant/Secondary
Joe Alley	Coaching Assistant
Josh Constant	Coaching Assistant
Carter Sheridan	Coaching Assistant
Adam Zimmer	Coaching Assistant

HOW THE TEAM WAS BUILT

Just how new was the Saints team assembled for the 2006 season? Here's a break-down of the players by year of joining the team.

1999
FREE AGENT
DE **Willie Whitehead** (FA)

2000
DRAFT
LS **Kevin Houser** (7)
FREE AGENTS
WR **Joe Horn** (UFA-KC)
CB **Fred Thomas** (UFA-Sea)

2001
DRAFT
RB **Deuce McAllister** (1)

FREE AGENTS
K **John Carney** (UFA-SD)

S **Steve Gleason** (FA)
WR **Michael Lewis** (FA)

2002
DRAFT
DE **Charles Grant** (1b)

2003
DRAFT
T **John Stinchcomb** (2)
G **Montrae Holland** (4)

2004
DRAFT
DE **Will Smith** (1)
WR **Devery Henderson** (2a)

DT **Rodney Leisle** (5a)
FB **Mike Karney** (5b)

FREE AGENTS
LB **Terrence Melton** (FA)
G/T **Jamar Nesbit** (UFA-Jax)
RB **Aaron Stecker** (UFA-TB)
DT **Brian Young** (UFA-StL)

TRADES
CB **Jason Craft** (Jax)
CB **Mike McKenzie** (GB)

2005
DRAFT
T **Jammal Brown** (1)
S **Josh Bullocks** (2)
LB **Alfred Fincher** (3)

2006
DRAFT
RB **Reggie Bush** (1)
G **Jahri Evans** (5a)
T **Zach Streif** (7a)
WR **Marques Colston** (7b)

FREE AGENTS
RB **Jamaal Branch** (FA)
QB **Drew Brees** (UFA-SD)

S **Jay Bellamy** (FA)
TE **Mark Campbell** (UFA-Buf)
DE **Josh Cooper** (FA)
K **Billy Cundiff** (FA)
LB **Scott Fujita** (UFA-Dal)
G/C **Jonathan Goodwin** (UFA-NYJ)
WR **Jamal Jones** (FA)
QB **Jamie Martin** (UFA-STL)
TE **Billy Miller** (FA)
TE **John Owens** (FA)
S **Omar Stoutmire** (UFA-Was)

TRADES
C **Jeff Faine** (Cle)
S **Bryan Scott** (Atl)
LB **Scott Shanle** (Dal)
DT **Hollis Thomas** (Phi)

WAIVERS
NT **Antwan Lake** (Atl)
T **Rob Petitti** (Dal)
DB **DeJuan Groce** (StL)
CB **Curtis Deloatch** (NYG)
WR **Terrance Copper** (Dal)

NEW ORLEANS SAINTS 2006 HONORS AND AWARDS

Pro Football Weekly/PFWA Executive of the Year
Executive Vice President/GM Mickey Loomis

Pro Football Weekly/PFWA Coach of the Year
Sean Payton

Associated Press Coach of the Year
Sean Payton

NFL Motorola Coach of the Year
Sean Payton

NFL FedEx Air Player of the Year
QB Drew Brees

NFL Walter Payton Man of the Year
QB Drew Brees

AFC-NFC Pro Bowl
QB Drew Brees
LT Jammal Brown
DE Will Smith

Associated Press All-Pro Team
QB Drew Brees
LT Jammal Brown
FB Mike Karney (second team)

Ed Block Courage Award
RB Deuce McAllister

NFC Rookie of the Month, October
WR Marques Colston

NFC Rookie of the Month, December
RB Reggie Bush

NFC Special Teams Player of the Month, September
K John Carney

NFC Offensive Player of the Week, Week 9
QB, Drew Brees

NFC Offensive Player of the Week, Week 13
RB, Reggie Bush

NFC Offensive Player of the Week, Week 14
QB Drew Brees

NFC Special Teams Player of the Week, Week 5
RB/PR Reggie Bush

NFC Defensive Player of the Week, Week 3
LB Scott Fujita

FedEx Air Player of the Week, Week 9
QB Drew Brees

FedEx Air Player of the Week, Week 12
QB Drew Brees

FedEx Air Player of the Week, Week 14
QB Drew Brees

FedEx Ground Player of the Week, Week 5
RB Deuce McAllister

NFL Diet Pepsi Rookie of the Week, Week 1
RB Reggie Bush

NFL Motorola Coach of the Week, Week 6
Head Coach Sean Payton

NFL Motorola Coach of the Week, Week 14
Head Coach Sean Payton

NEW ORLEANS SAINTS
2006 CHARITABLE DONATIONS

Since they came to town forty years ago, the Saints have been a vital partner for New Orleans charities. In the wake of Hurricane Katrina, that tradition only grew stronger. Below is a list of the major beneficiaries from the 2006 season.

Organizations and agencies that received funds from the New Orleans Saints Hurricane Katrina Fund

United Way of Greater New Orleans
Acorn Institute
Rebuilding Together
Catholic Charities
Dryades YMCA
Family Service

Hispanic Apostolate
Jewish Community Center
Kingsley House
Second Harvest Food Bank
Council on Alcohol and Drug Abuse
   (CADA)

Some of the organizations and agencies that received monetary donations from the New Orleans Saints in 2006

Audubon Institute
Bridge House
Preservation Resource Center

Boy Scouts of America
Crohn's and Colitis Foundation
Hispanic Chamber of Commerce

Southeast Louisiana Red Cross

Hispanic Heritage Foundation

Toys for Tots

McDonough 15 School

New Orleans Police and Justice
Foundation

Archbishop Rummel High School

The Jefferson Chamber of Commerce

The Legacy Donor Foundation

Fellowship of Christian Athletes

American Heart Association

Autism Speaks

Loyola University

Archbishop Shaw High School

New Orleans Museum of Art

Volunteers of America

Junior Achievement

Over 5,000 other charities, schools, churches, foundations, and festivals received in-kind donations from the Saints in 2006.

NEW ORLEANS SAINTS 2006
PLAYER APPEARANCES

What the Saints organization and players contribute to New Orleans can't just be measured by the size of their checkbooks. As an inspiration to all of us, especially kids, those players make ample use of their time to help put a smile on people's faces. Below is a list of all major player appearances from the 2006 season.

Friday, August 26
Players donate twenty-five motorized scooters, ten mountain bikes, eight color televisions, and five fans to the Boys & Girls Club in Jackson, Mississippi.

Tuesday, September 5
RB Reggie Bush participates in "Feed the Children" to bring two tractor trailers full of food and personal-care items to 800 families in the Garden District.

Saints WR Corps agrees to participate in the "Catches for CADA" program. CADA receives a donation for every catch made by the Saints receivers.

Tuesday, September 12
G Jahri Evans, T Ben Archibald, and QB Jason Fife help pick up trash outside of Tad Gormley Stadium to get it ready for prep football.

Tuesday, September 19

The New Orleans Saints organization donates $100,000 to NFL Youth Education Town (YET) center, and players and staff participate in the grand reopening of the youth center.

WR Joe Horn speaks to the TD Club of New Orleans.

Saturday, September 23

QB Drew Brees and RB Deuce McAllister host a "Cocktail for Katrina" fundraiser.

Saints host a Junior Player Development Jamboree for local teams, and participants help clean up Willie Hall Playground.

Monday, September 25

Saints reopen the Superdome and host the Atlanta Falcons on *Monday Night Football*.

Tuesday, September 26

Deuce McAllister and Drew Brees participate in the *Best Damn Sports Show Period* Sports Clinic at Taylor Playground.

Tuesday, October 3

WR Joe Horn visits St. Pius X School in Lakeview.

KR Michael Lewis visits McMain High School in New Orleans.

QB Drew Brees speaks to the TD Club of New Orleans.

Friday, October 6–Sunday, October 8

Saints have seven-year-old cancer patient Jonnie Shirley attend practice and meet the entire team with his family. The family is given tickets to the game by Coach

Payton, and Jonnie is given the game ball in the locker room following the victory over the Buccaneers.

Tuesday, October 10
Thirty Saints players and staff help landscape and paint the Priestley School of Architecture and Construction in uptown New Orleans as part of the 2006 Hometown Huddle with the United Way.

LS Kevin Houser speaks to the TD Club of New Orleans.

Saturday, October 14–Sunday, October 15
Saints host eight-year-old Cameron Steib and his family for a memorable weekend attending practice, meeting the team, and being junior captain for the game. Cameron is given the game ball in the locker room following the victory over the Eagles.

Tuesday, October 24
S Bryan Scott visits William J. Fischer Elementary Charter School on the Westbank.

LB Danny Clarke visits Martin Behrman Elementary School on the Westbank.

LB Scott Fujita visits Marie Riviere Elementary in Metairie.

G Jamar Nesbit speaks to a youth football team at Covington Recreation Department.

KR Michael Lewis speaks to the TD Club of New Orleans.

LS Kevin Houser speaks at the United Way Kickoff at Michoud Plant.

Tuesday, October 31

DE Charles Grant visits Our Lady of the Lake School in Mandeville.

WR Marques Colston, LB Terrence Melton, and LB E. J. Kuale visit Salmen High School in Slidell.

RB Aaron Stecker and FB Mike Karney visit St. Christopher Elementary School in Metairie.

Tuesday, November 7

OT Ben Archibald, OT Jon Stinchcomb, and OT Zach Strief visit Ethel Schoeffner Elementary School in Destrehan.

CB Mike McKenzie visits Lafayette Academy Charter School in New Orleans.

Tuesday, November 14

FB Corey McIntyre visits Edna Karr High School on the Westbank.

DT Rodney Leisle and DT Brian Young visit the pediatric ward at Ochsner Hospital.

LB Scott Fujita speaks to the TD Club of New Orleans.

Tuesday, November 21

TE Ernie Conwell visits Roosevelt Middle School in Metairie with CADA.

Twenty Saints players and staff give away 1,000 Thanksgiving turkey baskets funded by the players to needy families at the Dryades YMCA.

Tuesday, November 28

WR Joe Horn and KR Michael Lewis visit Ascension of Our Lord School in LaPlace.

FB Mike Karney visits the pediatric ward at Ochsner Hospital.

QB Drew Brees hosts the Brees Gridiron Classic at the Saints facility. Four youth teams play in a jamboree in the indoor facility and at halftime of the game versus the 49ers.

RB Deuce McAllister speaks to the TD Club of New Orleans.

Wednesday, November 29
WR Joe Horn visits Ochsner Hospital to see a Rummel football player who suffered a stroke.

Monday, December 4
RB Deuce McAllister hosts a holiday "Shop with a Jock" at Wal-Mart.

Tuesday, December 5
T Jon Stinchcomb and T Zach Strief visit the pediatric ward at Ochsner Hospital.

G Jahri Evans and T Zach Strief visit Martin Luther King Jr. Elementary School.

Tuesday, December 12
TE Billy Miller and TE John Owens visit the pediatric ward at Ochsner Hospital.

DE Charles Grant speaks to the TD Club of New Orleans.

Thursday, December 14
LB Danny Clarke hosts a holiday "Shop with a Jock" at Wal-Mart.

Tuesday, December 19
RB Deuce McAllister participates in "Take an NFL Player to School" at Christian Brothers School in City Park.

K John Carney hosts "Kick for Kids," buying seventy-five underprivileged kids two pairs of shoes and school supplies.

K Billy Cundiff visits the pediatric ward at Ochsner Hospital.

QB Drew Brees renovates the Children's Hospital van for the kids to be transported around town.

Friday, December 22

QB Drew Brees and CB Mike McKenzie give away 300 bikes bought by the Saints to area youth.

Friday, December 29

Saints have eight-year-old patient Caleb Garrard attend practice and meet the entire team with his family.

Friday, January 5

Saints have seven-year-old cancer patient Ja'Kyron Ladner attend practice and meet the entire team with his family. He also serves as the tee retriever at the playoff game.

In addition to "official" team-related charitable causes and appearances, every 2006 player spent time working in the community. Although the list of charities and endeavors on which players work is too great to mention here, a representative few include:

Mike McKenzie's 34 WAYS Foundation, which provides much-needed guidance to inner-city youths. It promotes not just sports but also academic mentoring programs that build character, teach discipline, and encourage good health and education.

Deuce McAllister's CATCH 22 Foundation, which supports many causes dear to him. Each year he hosts a highly successful golf tournament that benefits Children's Hospital.

Drew Brees's foundation helps provide scholarships to academically worthy students who otherwise might have their academic careers cut short due to financial hardship.

And before Hurricane Katrina, Steve Gleason led a very special team of volunteers who helped students actually write and then publish their own books. This activity follows through on Steve's belief that nothing is impossible. After Katrina, Steve saw a more basic need and organized efforts to buy and fill school bags with the supplies young students need to get their education back on track.

U.S. SENATE RESOLUTION 585
109th CONGRESS
2d Session
S. RES. 585

Commending the New Orleans Saints of the National Football League for winning their *Monday Night Football* game on Monday, September 25, 2006, by a score of 23 to 3.

IN THE SENATE OF THE UNITED STATES

SEPTEMBER 26, 2006

Ms. LANDRIEU submitted the following resolution; which was referred to the Committee on Commerce, Science, and Transportation

RESOLUTION

Commending the New Orleans Saints of the National Football League for winning their *Monday Night Football* game on Monday, September 25, 2006, by a score of 23 to 3.

Whereas the City of New Orleans and the State of Louisiana and the Gulf Coast were severely impacted by Hurricane Katrina on August 29, 2005, and the subsequent levee breaks which occurred;

Whereas southwestern Louisiana and the State of Louisiana were severely impacted by Hurricane Rita on September 24, 2005;

Whereas the New Orleans Saints and the Louisiana Superdome have always been special symbols of pride to the City of New Orleans and to the State of Louisiana;

Whereas, due to the leadership and hard work of the men and women who rebuilt the Superdome, as well as to the partnership of the National Football League, the State of Louisiana, and the Federal Emergency Management Agency, the Louisiana Superdome was able to reopen on Monday, September 25, 2006—13 months since the last New Orleans Saints home game was played there;

Whereas the return of the New Orleans Saints to the Louisiana Superdome serves as a symbol of hope for the great rebuilding of the City of New Orleans, the State of Louisiana, and the Gulf Coast region;

Whereas the City of New Orleans and the State of Louisiana showed its pride and support for the New Orleans Saints with an attendance of 70,003 fans at the September 25, 2006, game;

Whereas the New Orleans Saints won their first game in the Louisiana Superdome since Hurricanes Katrina and Rita by defeating the Atlanta Falcons, 23 to 3;

Whereas with the win over the Atlanta Falcons on Monday, September 25, 2006, the New Orleans Saints improve their record for the 2006–2007 season to a total of 3 wins and 0 losses, matching its win total from the 2005–2006 season and is 1 of just 6 National Football League teams with a record of 3 wins and 0 losses;

Whereas Head Coach Sean Payton led the New Orleans Saints to win their first 3 games of the 2006–2007 season and showed his appreciation to the City of New Orleans by giving the game ball to the city;

Whereas wide receiver Devery Henderson scored a touchdown on an 11-yard run in the game;

Whereas cornerback Curtis Deloach scored a touchdown following the blocked punt by Steve Gleason;

Whereas placekicker John Carney kicked 3 field goals in the game;

Whereas the New Orleans Saints defense held the Atlanta Falcons to 229 total yards in the game and had 5 sacks on the quarterback;

Whereas quarterback Drew Brees completed 20 of 28 pass attempts for a total of 191 yards in the game;

Whereas running back Deuce McAllister had 81 rushing yards and running back Reggie Bush had 53 rushing yards in the game;

Whereas the entire team and organization should be commended for their work together over the past 13 months;

Whereas the New Orleans Saints have demonstrated their excellence in athletics and have shown their commitment to the City of New Orleans and to the State of Louisiana through their hard work and sportsmanship; and

Whereas, with the triumphant return of the New Orleans Saints, the City of New Orleans and the State of Louisiana have proven to be open for business and ready to continue the recovery of the city, state, and region: Now, therefore, be it

Resolved, That the Senate commends the New Orleans Saints of the National Football League for winning their Monday, September 25, 2006, National Football League game with the Atlanta Falcons, by a score of 23 to 3.

LAGNIAPPE

HISTORY OF THE FLEUR-DE-LIS

The fleur-de-lis represents a stylized lily or lotus flower, and the literal English translation of fleur-de-lis is "flower of the lily." French royalty used it as their symbol, and in that sense it was used to signify light and life. It was a symbol of perfection. One legend tells that an angel gave a golden lily to Clovis, the Merovingian king of the Franks, to commemorate his purification upon converting to Christianity. Another legend says that Clovis adopted the symbol when water lilies showed him safe passage across a river, thus giving him success in battle.

During the twelfth century, King Louis VI placed the fleur-de-lis on his shield (some sources claim it was Louis VII). It was the first time the symbol had been used by French royalty. English kings later used it on their coats of arms to back up their claims to the throne of France. In the fourteenth century, the fleur-de-lis was often sewn onto the family insignia on a knight's surcoat, which was worn over his coat of mail, thus the term "coat of arms." Though originally intended for the purpose of identification in battle, the coats of arms evolved into a system of social-status markers when King Edmund IV founded the Heralds' College.

The fleur-de-lis found its way into many other historical moments over the centuries. When Joan of Arc led French troops to victory over the English in support of the Dauphin, Charles VII, she carried a white banner that showed God blessing the French royal emblem.

The Roman Catholic Church made the lily a special emblem of the Virgin

Mary. The fleur-de-lis has also been used to represent the Holy Trinity, thanks to its three "petals." The symbol also bears a resemblance to a spearhead, which many military units, including the U.S. Army, have used to symbolize martial power and strength.

And in 1966, the fleur-de-lis was adopted and taken into battle once again, this time by the New Orleans Saints.

HISTORY OF "WHO DAT?"

In proper English, one might say it more like, "Who are they who believe that they might beat those Saints?"

Although there are many versions of the story of how the chant came to be, the most popular is that it began in the cheering section of the St. Augustine Purple Knights, a predominantly African-American Catholic boys' high school in New Orleans. Always a football powerhouse, St. Aug's fans began chanting "Who dat? Who dat? Who dat say they gonna beat St. Aug, who dat?"

Those same fans most likely brought the chant with them to the Superdome during the Bum Phillips era. It was quickly accepted by Saints fans. Since then, it has been used in various recordings, including one by Aaron Neville. It also inspired an official fan club, the Who Dat Fan Club. Saints fans are often referred to as Who Dats and a Saints fan will often save energy and breath by shortening the chant to just a random "Who Dat!" shouted at an opponent or its fans.

THE SAINTS HALL OF FAME

Located in Kenner, LA, the Saints Hall of Fame was founded by Kenner mayor Aaron Broussard and local sports personality Ken Trahan. The museum is not officially a part of the Saints organization and is one of only two team halls of fame in the NFL. Green Bay has the other. But the Saints Hall of Fame is even more unique; it is the only hall created by the fans for the fans. Items on display there include the ball John Gilliam carried for a touchdown on the opening kick in the very first Saints game and the shoe Tom Dempsey wore when he kicked his record-setting field goal. Today you will find a life-size cutout of Reggie Bush. Making the museum even more special are the personal items donated by fans, which include programs, tickets, and memorabilia.

"WHEN THE SAINTS GO MARCHING IN"

Lyrics: Traditional

We are trav'ling in the footsteps
Of those who've gone before
And we'll all be reunited
On a new and sunlit shore

Oh, when the saints go marching in
Oh, when the saints go marching in
Lord, how I want to be in that number
When the saints go marching in

And when the sun refuse to shine
And when the sun refuse to shine
Lord, how I want to be in that number
When the sun refuse to shine

And when the moon turns red with blood
And when the moon turns red with blood
Lord, how I want to be in that number
When the moon turns red with blood

LAGNIAPPE

Oh, when the trumpet sounds its call
Oh, when the trumpet sounds its call
Lord, how I want to be in that number
When the trumpet sounds its call

Some say this world of trouble
Is the only one we need
But I'm waiting for that morning
When the new world is revealed

ACKNOWLEDGMENTS

AS I WRITE this, Abbe Garfinkel is less than two weeks from finally moving back into her house. Michelle Babineaux is drumming up business for Michaul's and raising her three–year-old son. Pam Randazza is ordering new merchandise for her store and filling online orders. Jack Catilanatto is back in the insurance business. Daniel Garroway is finishing the sixth grade, looking forward to the seventh, and is wearing his Deuce McAllister jersey.

Ken Trahan is active in local sports media and is keeping memories of the Saints alive at the Saints Hall of Fame. Quint Davis is cleaning up after Jazz Fest 2007. Kenny Wilkerson and Bobby Hebert are hosting their daily radio show on WWL. Billy Cundiff and Joe Horn are teammates in Atlanta. Fred McAfee retired from football but was brought back *again* by the Saints, this time to help players transition into and out of the NFL. Anthony Canatella is keeping

the peace. Lindy Boggs is restoring her centuries-old home in the French Quarter. Doug Thornton is managing the Superdome and working to bring events to the city. Mitch Landrieu is working to create and maintain jobs as lieutenant governor of Louisiana. Sammy Marten is running a comedy club in Memphis and looking for a ticket. To what, I am not exactly sure.

So many people helped me while I was creating this book, but there is not enough space to thank them all, so if you are reading this and don't see your name, I love you and the check is in the mail. I would like to thank Dave Dixon for making so many things happen during my lifetime and letting me know how they happened; Lindy Boggs for giving me a look into her life and her husband, Hale's; Jerry Daigle for being a good friend and occasional calming influence; Doug Thornton for sharing a story that deserves its own book—and a movie, too; Kenny Wilkerson, without whom I could never have written this book; Chris Park for taking a chance on me and keeping this alive when I was behind schedule; A. J. Sisco for working so hard to get many of the pictures in this book; Chris Myers for calling back at 1 a.m. (his time) to tell me he would help; Tanner Colby, who told me I could do this, then made me; Ralph Dominique, my sixth grade teacher at Lakeview School, for early guidance and inspiration; the Jesuit High School English department, with apologies if I have embarrassed them; and, of course, my mom and dad for more things than can be listed here; my brothers, Bert, Stephen, and Richard, for tolerating me.

I would especially like to thank every man who has ever worn a Saints uniform and every last Who Dat in the Who Dat Nation.

Special editorial assistance provided by H. Andrew Buchler III.